Property and Trust Law in Indonesia

Property and Trust Law in Indonesia

Eddy M. Leks

This book was originally published as a monograph in the International Encyclopaedia of Laws/Property and Trust Law.

Founding Editor: Roger Blanpain
General Editor: Frank Hendrickx
Volume Editors: Alain Verbeke & Vincent Sagaert

Wolters Kluwer

Published by:
Kluwer Law International B.V.
PO Box 316
2400 AH Alphen aan den Rijn
The Netherlands
E-mail: international-sales@wolterskluwer.com
Website: lrus.wolterskluwer.com

Sold and distributed in North, Central and South America by:
Wolters Kluwer Legal & Regulatory U.S.
7201 McKinney Circle
Frederick, MD 21704
United States of America
Email: customer.service@wolterskluwer.com

Sold and distributed in all other countries by:
Air Business Subscriptions
Rockwood House
Haywards Heath
West Sussex
RH16 3DH
United Kingdom
Email: international-customerservice@wolterskluwer.com

Printed on acid-free paper

ISBN 978-94-035-0134-5

e-Book: ISBN 978-94-035-0200-7
web-PDF: ISBN 978-94-035-0242-7

This title is available on www.kluwerlawonline.com

Printed in the United Kingdom.

The Author

Eddy Leks is the founder and managing partner of Leks&Co. With a legal career in mind, he started his experience in the practice areas of general corporate/commercial and commercial dispute resolution. Later, he joined Hadiputranto, Hadinoto & Partners (HHP), an affiliated law office of Baker & McKenzie. There he worked in the capital market, general corporate/commercial, taxation, foreign investment, and customs division. He left HHP to join PT Lippo Karawaci Tbk, one of the largest property and real estate development and investment companies in Indonesia, where he rose to become a senior legal manager. His main responsibilities were to manage the company's general corporate/commercial issues, build-operate-transfer projects, and acquisition of shares and assets for property projects. He was one of the company's youngest legal managers when he joined.

Eddy Leks specializes in real estate law, mergers acquisition and commercial dispute resolution. His writings have been published in many prominent publications locally and internationally, such as *Forbes Indonesia*, *Property&Bank*, *Kontan*, *LAWASIA Journal*, the *International Bar Association Real Estate* Newsletter, *Jurnal Hukum Bisnis*, The Institutional Real Estate Letter – *Asia Pacific*, and Indonesian chapter of *The Real Estate Review*, published by *Law Business Research*. He is also invited to speak at many events, locally and internationally, on real estate law, foreign investment, bankruptcy, lease agreement, and other law matters. He was involved as Chairman of Analysis and Evaluation of Laws on Public Housing, a programme by National Legal Development Body, to provide input and report to be used by the government of Indonesia to rectify conflicting regulations and to facilitate housings for the low-income communities.

Eddy Leks is recommended by Asialaw Profiles, Legal 500, Chambers and Partners in the field of real estate in Indonesia. He is also recommended on corporate and M&A by Asialaw Profiles and Legal 500. The latter also recommends him on commercial dispute resolution. He was nominated as one of the finalists to receive BMW Award Managing Partner of the Year by ALB Indonesia Law Awards 2015. Further, he is also awarded as Asialaw Leading Lawyer and Euromoney Expert Guides in the field of construction and real estate. He is identified as the first and the only Indonesian lawyer by Who's Who Legal 2014 in the field of real estate. Further, he is also awarded as mergers and acquisition lawyer of the year by Finance Monthly Global Awards 2014. Eddy holds a certificate in international trade and finance (CITF). In addition, he holds two postgraduate degrees in Law from Universitas Gadjah Mada, Indonesia and the University of London, London with a specialization on International Dispute Resolution.

Table of Contents

The Author 3

List of Abbreviations 9

General Introduction 11

§1. General Background of the Country 11

I. Geography 11
II. Cultural Situation 11
III. Political System 12

§2. Legal Background of the Country 13

I. Legal Family or Tradition 13
A. Pre-independence 13
1. Vereenigde Oost Indische Compagnie Era (VOC) (1602–1799) 13
2. Dutch East Indies Government Era 14
a. Besluiten Regerings (BR) Era (1814–1855) 14
b. Regerings Reglement Era (1855–1926) 14
c. Indische Staatsregeling Era (1926–1942) 15
d. Japan Era (Osamu Seirei) 16
B. Post-Independence 17
1. Old Order 17
a. 1945–1949 Era 17
b. 1949–1950 Era 17
c. 1950–1959 Era 18
d. 1959–1965 Era 18
2. New Order 18
3. Reform Order 19
II. Relation and Hierarchy Between the Sources of Law 19
A. Law and Its Relation 19
B. Sources of Law 19

§3. Introduction to the Law of Property and Trust 21

I. Historical Origins and Evolution 21

II. The Concept of Ownership 23
A. Unity and Fragmentation 23
B. Immovable and Real Property (see also Part I) 23
C. Movable and Personal Property (see also Part II) 26
III. Estate and Patrimony 26
A. Unity and Fragmentation 26
B. Trust and Fiduciary Mechanisms (see also Parts IV and V) 27
IV. Possession and Title 28

Part I. Immovable Property and Real Property 31

Chapter 1. General Classification 31

Chapter 2. Legal Interests 32

Chapter 3. Equitable Interests 33

Chapter 4. Limited Interests 35

§1. Usufruct 35

§2. Building and Planting Rights 35

§3. Leasehold Interests: Chattels Real (see also Part II) 35

§4. Emphyteusis and Rent Charge 35

§5. Use and Habitation/Occupation 36

§6. Easements and Profits 36

§7. Licences 36

§8. Restrictive Covenants 37

Chapter 5. Security Interests (see also Parts II, IV, and V) 38

Chapter 6. Joint Ownership 40

§1. Joint Ownership of Immovable Property 40

I. In General 40
II. Co-ownership Applied to Apartment Buildings 40

§2. Joint Ownership over Movable Property 41

Chapter 7. Neighbourhood and Urban Problems 42

Chapter 8. Agrarian Problems 43

Part II. Movable Property and Personal Property/Chattels 45

Chapter 1. General Classification 45

§1. Tangible Movable Property and Choses in Possession 45

§2. Intangible Movable Property and Choses in Action 47

§3. Funds (Capital; Investment Fund) 47

§4. Chattels Personal and Chattels Real 49

Chapter 2. Legal Interests 52

Chapter 3. Equitable Interests 54

Chapter 4. Security Interests 55

Part III. Acquisition of Property Rights 57

Chapter 1. Transfer of Property by Contract Inter Vivos 57

Chapter 2. Transfer of Property by Death 58

Chapter 3. Possession 59

Chapter 4. Accession 61

Chapter 5. Appropriation 62

Chapter 6. Expropriation 64

Chapter 7. Insolvency 67

Part IV. Trust and Fiduciary Mechanisms 69

Chapter 1. Administration of Property. Fiducia Cum Amico 69

Chapter 2. Security. Fiducia Cum Creditore (see also Parts I, II and V) 71

Part V. Security 83

Table of Contents

Chapter 1. Securities in Immovable Property (see also Parts I and IV) 83

§1. Privileges, Liens, Charges 83

§2. Mortgage 84

Chapter 2. Securities in Movable Property (see also Parts II and IV) 96

§1. Privileges, Liens, Charges 96

§2. Pledge 97

§3. Retention Right, Compensation 103

§4. Delegation, Direct Claim (Possibly Created by Statute Law to Claim Payment Directly from the Debtor of One's Debt) 104

Selected Bibliography 105

Table of Cases 107

Index 109

List of Abbreviations

AB	Algemene Bepalingen van Wetgeving voor Indonesia
Agrarian Law	Law Number 5 of 1960 on Basic Provisions of Principles of Agrarian
Bankruptcy Law	Law Number 37 of 2004 on Bankruptcy and Postponement of Obligation of Debt Payment
BOT	Build, Operate, and Transfer
BR	*Besluiten Regerings*
BTO	Build, Transfer, and Operate
Building Law	Law Number 28 of 2002 on Building
BW	*Burgerlijk Wetboek*
Camat	Head of District
Capital Investment Law	Law Number 25 of 2007 on Capital Investment
Company Law	Law Number 40 of 2007 on Limited Liability Company
Condominium Law	Law Number 20 of 2011 on Condominium
Constitution 1945	Constitution of the Republic of Indonesia of 1945, lastly amended in Annual Plenary of MPR in 2002
Constitution 1950	Temporary Constitution of 1950
Constitution RIS	Constitution of the Republic of Indonesia Union
Corruption Law	Eradication of Corruption Criminal Offense as amended by Law Number 20 of 2011
DPD	Regional Representative Council (*Dewan Perwakilan Daerah*)
DPR	People's Representative Council (*Dewan Perwakilan Rakyat*)
Fiduciary Security Law	Law Number 42 of 1999 on Fiduciary Security
Flight Law	Law Number 15 of 1993 on Flight

List of Abbreviations

Foundation Law	Law Number 16 of 2001 on Foundation as lastly amended by Law Number 28 of 2004
GR 27/2014	Government Regulation Number 27 of 2014 on Management of State/Regional-owned Goods
Housing Law	Law Number 1 of 2011 on Housing and Residential Area
ICC	Indonesian Civil Code
IS	*Indische Staatsregeling*
Land Procurement Law	Law Number 2 of 2012 on Land Procurement for Public Interest
Land Registration Reg	Government Regulation Number 24 of 1997 on Land Registration
Land Revocation Law	Law Number 20 of 1961 on Revocation of Rights of Land and Properties Over It
Money Laundering Law	Law Number 8 of 2010 on Prevention and Eradication of Money Laundering Criminal Offense
Mortgage Law	Law Number 4 of 1996 on Mortgage and Land-Related Objects
MPR	People's Consultative Assembly (*Majelis Permusyawaratan Rakyat*)
MR 3/1997	Regulation of State Minister of Agrarian/ Chairman of National Land Office Number 3 of 1997 on Implementing Provisions of Government Regulation Number 24 of 1997 on Land Registration
P3SRS	Association of Owner and Tenant of Condominium Unit
Pancasila	Five Principles
PPAT	Land Conveyancing Officer (*Pejabat Pembuat Akta Tanah*)
President	President of the Republic of Indonesia
RR	*Regerings Reglement*
SOE Law	Law Number 19 of 2003 on State-owned Enterprises
VOC	Vereenigde Oost Indische Compagnie
WvK	*Wetboek van Koophandel*
WvS	*Wetboek van Strafrecht*

General Introduction

§1. General Background of the Country

I. Geography

1. Indonesia is a vast equatorial archipelago of 17,000 islands extending 5,150 kilometres (3,200 miles) east to west, between the Indian and Pacific Oceans in Southeast Asia. The largest islands are Sumatra, Java, Kalimantan (Indonesian Borneo), Sulawesi, and the Indonesian part of New Guinea (known as Papua or Irian Jaya). Islands are mountainous with dense rain forests, and some have active volcanoes. Most of the smaller islands belong to larger groups, like the Moluccas (Spice Islands).[1]

2. Indonesia, the world's fourth most populous nation, has 86% Muslims – and the largest Islamic country, though it is a secular state. Indonesians are separated by seas and clustered on islands. The largest cluster is on Java, with some 130 million inhabitants (60% of the country's population) on an island that is the size of New York State. Sumatra, much larger than Java, has less than a third of its people. Ethnically the country is highly diverse, with over 580 languages and dialects – but only 13 have more than 1 million speakers.[2]

II. Cultural Situation

3. Indonesia's size and ethnic diversity has made national identity problematic and debated. Identity is defined at many levels: by Indonesian citizenship; by recognition of the flag, national anthem, and certain other songs; by recognition of national holidays; and by education about Indonesia's history and the Five Principles: belief in one supreme God; just and civilized humanitarianism; Indonesian unity; popular sovereignty governed by wise policies arrived at through deliberation and representation; and social justice for all Indonesian people on which the nation is based. Much of this is instilled through schools and media, both of which have been closely regulated by the government during most of the years of independence. The nation's history has been focused upon resistance to colonialism and communism by national heroes and leaders who are

1. At http://travel.nationalgeographic.com/travel/countries/indonesia-facts/, accessed mid-year of 2017.
2. *Ibid.*

enshrined in street names. Glories of past civilizations are recognized, although archaeological remains are mainly of Javanese principalities.[3]

4. The national motto, *Bhinneka Tunggal Ika*, is an old Javanese expression usually translated as 'unity in diversity'. The nation's official ideology, first formulated by President Sukarno in 1945, is the Pancasila or Five Principles.[4] Each ethnic group has had its own historical background. Within those histories, there were acculturations processes, whenever a strong foreign culture is intruding or pushing hard into each respective culture. Each traditional ethnic culture in Indonesia is different from other culture by two factors. First, many ethnic cultures had been different from each other since their respective basic prehistoric phase of development. Second, their ever-evolving traditional cultures develop the more specific characteristics due to different experiences in acculturation processes.[5]

5. Almost every ethnic group has its own style of dance, music, and visual arts traditionally handed down from generation to generation. Some of the dances, for instance, are so closely related in terms of technique and style, that they can be collapsed into something that might be called 'a family of dance styles'. These 'families' of dance styles are mostly concurrently identified by similar types of musical instruments used, as well as song styles.[6]

6. Within the present-day Indonesian nation, each ethnic group is allotted its distinct place. The ethnic, cultural heritage in general is considered a common national heritage of Indonesia. Cultural expressions of ethnic origin, as far as they are not in opposition to the agreed upon national philosophy of Indonesia, the Pancasila, are paid heed to and maintained with care. They are even considered as one among the providers of national identity, along with the newly formed cultural achievements. Reciprocal appraisal, or mutual appreciation, among the different ethnic groups is then a prerequisite for the present-day Indonesian nation.[7]

III. Political System

7. In accordance with the 1945 Constitution, the State of the Republic of Indonesia is a state with the organizational structure of a unitary state, in which state power is divided between the central government and the regional governments. The original power lies at the central government, whereas regional governments obtain their powers from the central government through the delegation of certain expressly specified powers.[8]

8. The executive branch consists of the president, the vice president, and the cabinet. Both the president and vice president are chosen by the Indonesian electorate

3. At http://www.everyculture.com/Ge-It/Indonesia.html, accessed mid-year of 2017.
4. Symbolism. http://www.everyculture.com/Ge-It/Indonesia.html, accessed mid-year of 2017.
5. 2 Edi Sedyawati, *KeIndonesiaan dalam Budaya*, p. 28 (1st edition. 2008).
6. *Ibid.*, p. 36.
7. *Ibid.*, p. 37.
8. Prof Dr Jimly Asshiddiqie, S.H., *The Constitutional Law of Indonesia*, p. 235 (1st edition. 2009).

through presidential elections. They serve for a term of five years that can be extended once by another term of five years when re-elected by the people.

9. The legislative branch is the People's Consultative Assembly (*Majelis Permusyawaratan Rakyat*, abbreviated MPR). It has the power to set or change the Constitution and appoints (or impeaches) the president. The MPR is a bicameral parliament that consists of the People's Representative Council (*Dewan Perwakilan Rakyat*, abbreviated DPR) and the Regional Representative Council (*Dewan Perwakilan Daerah*, abbreviated DPD).[9]

10. The highest court in Indonesia's judiciary system is the Supreme Court (*Mahkamah Agung*). It is the final Court of Appeal that deals with disputes between lower courts. A new court, established in 2003, is the Constitutional Court (*Mahkamah Konstitusi*), which monitors whether decisions made by the cabinet and parliament (MPR) are in line with the Indonesian Constitution. Most of the legal cases, however, are dealt with by the public courts, administrative courts, religious courts and military courts. A Judicial Commission (*Komisi Yudisial*) oversees the maintenance of honour, dignity, and behaviour of Indonesian judges.[10]

§2. Legal Background of the Country

I. Legal Family or Tradition

A. Pre-independence

1. Vereenigde Oost Indische Compagnie Era (VOC) (1602–1799)

11. VOC was established by the Dutch traders in 1602 with a purpose to prevent competition among traders buying spices from indigenous people so that they can get huge profits from European market.[11]

12. During a trade era in Indonesia, VOC is granted a special right by the Dutch government called *octrooi.* The right comprises monopoly of shipping and trade, right to declare a war, constitute the means for peaceful settlement and printing money. That special right results in the expansion of its colony to archipelago islands.[12]

13. In its effort to increase profit, VOC enforces rules from its country to be adhered by indigenous people. Those enforced rules are rules on trade that used to be implemented on merchant ships. Those rules are the same as ancient Dutch law that mostly are 'disciplinary law'.[13]

9. *Ibid.*
10. *Ibid.*
11. Mokhammad Najih, S.H., M.Hum and Soimin, S.H., M.H., *Pengantar Hukum Indonesia: Sejarah, Konsep Tata Hukum, dan Politik Hukum Indonesia*, p. 30 (revised edition. Setara Press 2014).
12. J.B. Daliyo, S.H., *Pengantar Hukum Indonesia*, p. 13 (Gramedia Pustaka Utama 1997).
13. *Ibid.*, p. 13.

14. When VOC was dissolved on 31 December 1799 by the Dutch government, the prevailing system of law derived its rule from the Netherlands and rules made by the ruling governor general in the territory of VOC as well as unwritten and written rules applicable for indigenous people, namely their own customary law.[14]

2. Dutch East Indies Government Era

a. Besluiten Regerings (BR) Era (1814–1855)

15. Since 1 January 1800, VOC's territories are taken over by the *Bataafsche Republiek* which then was changed into *Koninklijk Holand.* The archipelago suffers colonization by the Dutch government since then. To manage its territories, the absolute Dutch monarch appointed Daendels as governor general.[15]

16. During the era of BR, the king has absolute and highest authority on colonialized territories including absolute power against assets of other state. King's absolute power is also applicable to make and issue prevailing general rules called as *Algemene Verordening* or central rules. Central rules are king's decision and so they are called as *Koninklijk Besluit.*[16]

17. One thing to note is that in 1830, Dutch East Indies government has been successful in codifying the civil law. The promulgation of its codification was however made only on 1 October 1838. Then, for Dutch East Indies, a codification of civil law was also expected that will be applied for Dutch in accordance with the colonialized territories.[17]

b. Regerings Reglement Era (1855–1926)

18. There occurred an amendment of Netherlands' *Grondwet* in 1848 as a result of conflict of *de Staten General* (parliament) and King that ended with the victory of parliament to manage state's affairs. That victory changes the government system from constitutional monarchy to parliamentary constitutional monarch. Changes on *Grondwet* results in the changes over government and laws of Indonesia, especially provisions in Article 59 paragraph (I, II and IV) of *Grondwet* that states:[18]

> Para I: King has highest authority over colonialized territories and kingdom's assets over the part of the world.

14. *Ibid.*, p. 14.
15. Mokhammad Najih, S.H., M.Hum and Soimin, S.H., M.H., *Pengantar Hukum Indonesia: Sejarah, Konsep Tata Hukum, dan Politik Hukum Indonesia*, p. 31 (revised edition. Setara Press 2014).
16. J.B. Daliyo, S.H., *Pengantar Hukum Indonesia*, pp. 14–15 (Gramedia Pustaka Utama 1997).
17. *Ibid.*, p. 16.
18. Mokhammad Najih, S.H., M.Hum and Soimin, SH., M.H., *Pengantar Hukum Indonesia: Sejarah, Konsep Tata Hukum, dan Politik Hukum Indonesia*, p. 34 (revised edition. Setara Press 2014).

Para II: Rules on government's policy are stipulated through a law. Financial system is stipulated through a law.

Para IV: Matters related to colonialized territories and asset, when necessary, will be regulated through a law.

19. From the above-mentioned provisions, the diminishing power of the king over colonialized territories in Indonesia is clear. The rules governing colonialized territories are not only stipulated by the king through his *Koninklijk Besluit* but by the king and the parliament. The joint rules made by the king and the parliament are called *Regerings Reglement* (RR). In 1920, some provisions of RR were amended called as new RR, applicable between 1 January 1930 and 1926. The group of people as set forth in Article 75 of RR was amended from two groups to three groups, namely European, Foreign East, and Indonesia (indigenous).[19]

c. Indische Staatsregeling Era (1926–1942)

20. *Indische Staatsregeling* is a renewed RR and was applicable since 1 January 1926 through S.1925:415. The renewal of RR into IS was a result of change of Dutch East Indies government of the amendment of *Grond Wet* in 1922.[20]

21. During the IS era, the applicable system of law in Dutch East Indies was firstly written rules and unwritten rules (customary law) where their character was still pluralistic, especially private law. One can see it in Article 131 of IS. Nevertheless, it is also understood that Dutch East Indies opened possibilities for law unification for three groups of people in Dutch East Indies that is regulated under Article 163 of IS.[21]

22. J.B Daliyo in his book titled, *Pengantar Hukum Indonesia*, in pages 19–21, explains the applicable system of law for each group:

(1) Applicable laws for European group as set forth in Article 131 of IS are civil law, material criminal law, and procedural law:

  (a) Applicable civil law for European group is *Burgerlijk Wetboek* and *Wetboek van Koophandel* (BW and WvK) promulgated on 1 May 1848, using concordance principle.
  (b) Applicable material criminal law for European group is *Wetboek van Strafrecht* (WvS) promulgated on 1 January 1948 through S.1915:732.
  (c) The procedural law used in a court proceeding for European group is *Reglement op de Burgerlijk Rechtsvordering* for civil cases and *Reglement op de Strafvordering* promulgated through S.1847:52. Both were applicable for Java and Madura. The hierarchy of courts for European in Java and Madura is *Residentiegerecht*, *Raad van Justitie*, and *Hooggerechtshof.* Courts outside

19. J.B. Daliyo, S.H., *Pengantar Hukum Indonesia*, pp. 17–18 (Gramedia Pustaka Utama 1997).
20. *Ibid.*, p. 18.
21. *Ibid.*, pp. 18–19.

Java and Madura are stipulated under *Rechts Reglement Buitengewesten* through S.1927:227 for each of the regions.

(2) Applicable laws for indigenous people are unwritten customary laws. Nevertheless, if the Dutch East Indies government wishes otherwise, the customary law can be replaced by its issued ordinances (Article 131 paragraph 6 of IS). Thus, the applicability of customary law is not absolute. The circumstance has been proven with the issuance of various ordinances applicable to all groups:

(a) S.1933:48 jo. S.1938:2 on ship registration regulation;
(b) S.1933:108 on general regulation of cooperative association;
(c) S.1938:523 on loan of money;
(d) S.1938:524 on usury.

Applicable laws for indigenous people:

(a) S.1927:91 on indigenous cooperative;
(b) S.1931:33 on appointment of guardian in Java and Madura;
(c) S.1933:74 on Christian marriage in Java, Minahasa, and Amboina;
(d) S.1933:75 on regulation of census for Indonesian in Java, Madura, Minahasa, Amboina, Saparua, and Banda;
(e) S.1939:569 on *Andil* Airline.
(f) S.1939:570 on indigenous association.

(3) Applicable law for Foreign East:

(a) Their own civil law and criminal customary law as set forth in Article 11 of AB, in accordance with S.1855:79 (for all Foreign East groups);
(b) European group civil law applicable for Chinese Foreign East in Dutch East Indies through S.1924:557 and for West Borneo, the applicability of BW was through S.1925:92 on 1 September 1925;
(c) Applicable WvS since 1 January 1919, for material criminal law;
(d) Applicable procedural law for European group and applicable procedural law for indigenous group since in practice, both procedural laws were used in court for Foreign East group.

d. Japan Era (Osamu Seirei)

23. During the Japanese era, Dutch East Indies was divided into two, namely East Indonesia under Japanese Navy located in Makasar and West Indonesia under Japanese Army located in Jakarta. Rules governing the Dutch East Indies territories were made under Gun Seirei through Osamu Seirei.[22]

24. Osamu Seirei applies generally to run government. Osamu Kanrei as the implementing regulation regulates necessary matters to safeguard public order. Article 3 of Osamue Seirei Number 1 of 1942 states that 'all governmental bodies and their

22. J.B. Daliyo, S.H., *Pengantar Hukum Indonesia*, pp. 21–23 (Gramedia Pustaka Utama 1997).

powers, laws and regulations by the previous government, are validly acknowledged temporarily, as long as they do not conflict with the military rules'. Therefore, all regulations by Dutch East Indies were still applicable as positive law.[23]

B. Post-Independence

1. Old Order

a. 1945–1949 Era

25. After independence, Indonesia is a free nation without dependence on any parties. The applicable constitution as a basis to run a government was determined on 18 August 1945. The constitution was called as Constitution 1945.[24]

26. The applicable system of law during that era can be seen in Article II of Transitional Provision of Constitution 1945 that states, 'all state's bodies and existing regulations are applicable, as long as there are no replacement under this Constitution'. It means that all existing regulations since the era of Dutch colonization, Japanese era, are still valid.[25]

b. 1949–1950 Era

27. The era of 1945–1949 was not long because Netherlands invaded Indonesia through allied forces to reinforce the government's wheel of Dutch East Indies in Indonesia, causing an independence war. The independence war ended in December 1949 with the Round Table Conference in Den Haag caused change of administrative structure in Indonesia, from unitary state to federal state by enacting a Constitution of Republic of Indonesia Union (Constitution RIS).[26]

28. Article 192 of Constitution RIS states:

> regulations, laws and administrative provisions that are existed by the time this constitution is effective are still valid, not-amended, as regulations and provisions of RIS, during and as long as those regulations and provisions are not revoked, added or amended by a law and administrative provision by the power of this constitution.

---

23. Mokhammad Najih, S.H., M.Hum and Soimin, S.H., M.H., *Pengantar Hukum Indonesia: Sejarah, Konsep Tata Hukum, dan Politik Hukum Indonesia*, p. 36 (revised edition. Setara Press 2014).
24. J.B. Daliyo, S.H., *Pengantar Hukum Indonesia*, pp. 23–24 (Gramedia Pustaka Utama 1997).
25. *Ibid.*, p. 24.
26. Mokhammad Najih, S.H., M.Hum and Soimin, S.H., M.H., *Pengantar Hukum Indonesia: Sejarah, Konsep Tata Hukum, dan Politik Hukum Indonesia*, pp. 40–41 (revised edition. Setara Press 2014).

29. This federal state lasted for eight months. Through Federal Law Number 7 of 1950, Constitution RIS was replaced by Temporary Constitution of 1950 (Constitution 1950) that brought back the Unitary State of the Republic of Indonesia.[27]

c. 1950–1959 Era

30. All regulations applicable during this era are all laws and regulations that are declared applicable under Article 142 of Constitution 1950, along with new regulations formed by the state during the era.[28]

d. 1959–1965 Era

31. The Constitution 1959 was only valid until 4 July 1959 since Presidential Decree of 5 July 1959 has declared that the Constitution 1950 is no longer applicable. Therefore, the applicable constitution after 1959 to date is Constitution 1945.[29]

32. An important law during this era was Law Number 5 of 1960 on Basic Provisions of Principles of Agrarian ('Agrarian Law') declaring that most of the clauses in Book II of Indonesian Civil Code (ICC) were no longer valid.[30]

33. This era was also called as Led Democracy initiated by the President Soekarno, as an effort to resolve difference on ideology and to complete revolution, but in practice, tended to an authoritarian pattern. The peak was the occurrence of coup d'état by Indonesian Communist Party on 30 September 1965, which was a failure.[31]

2. New Order

34. After the failed coup d'état, and also after the issuance of Instruction Letter on 11 March 1966 which was normally called as 'Supersemar', a new era has begun, which is also named as 'new order'. New order government intends to realize Pancasila and Constitution 1945 purely and consequently.[32]

35. In order to actualize this new policy, new order government formed a long-term development in 1969 with a five-year series, after previously promulgated law on foreign investment in 1967 and law on domestic investment in 1968.[33]

36. Unfortunately, the implementation of ideas to actualize pure and consistent Pancasila and Constitution 1945 was not achieved by new order. In contrast, the new order was in fact violated those prevailing laws and regulations for power.[34]

---

27. *Ibid.*, pp. 40–41.
28. J.B. Daliyo, S.H., *Pengantar Hukum Indonesia*, p. 25 (Gramedia Pustaka Utama 1997).
29. *Ibid.*, p. 25.
30. Mokhammad Najih, S.H., M.Hum and Soimin, S.H., M.H., *Pengantar Hukum Indonesia: Sejarah, Konsep Tata Hukum, dan Politik Hukum Indonesia*, p. 43 (revised edition. Setara Press 2014).
31. *Ibid.*, p. 44.
32. *Ibid.*, p. 44.
33. *Ibid.*, p. 45.
34. *Ibid.*, p. 48.

37. Decline of administrative system built during new order reached its peak along with global financial crisis impacting Indonesia and Asian countries. This event aroused young generation in Indonesia to fix the system through a reformation initiated by students' movement and intellectuals of Indonesia to impeach President Soeharto from his presidency. Reform movement was successful in its demand that caused President Soeharto to resign on 21 May 1998.[35]

3. Reform Order

38. Success of reform movement was as a result of united passion from young generation to demand political reform in Indonesia's administrative system. This era saw an amendment of Constitution 1945 for four times, from 65 clauses to 197 clauses. From that number, 20 clauses were intact, 43 clauses were amended, and 128 clauses were additional provisions. The amendment ended with the fourth amendment in an Annual Plenary of MPR in 2002.[36]

II. Relation and Hierarchy Between the Sources of Law

A. Law and Its Relation

39. Law is a power to control and enforce. For example, law governs relationship between creditor who lends money and debtor who borrows money and it is conducted by establishing laws and regulations. People who lend money to others are entitled to request their money and the other party is obligated to fulfil it. That type of relationship is called as legal relationship.[37]

40. Legal relationship consists of two aspects, right and obligation. One normally uses law in two sense, namely to state that a regulation governing relationship between two persons or more. This type of law is called an objective law. It is applicable for public, not for a specific subject. The other is to state relationship governed by the objective law, where one party has the right, and the other has an obligation. This type of law is called as subjective law since in this matter, a law is linked to a specific person, specific subject.[38]

B. Sources of Law

41. Sources of law can be understood as materials used as a basis by the court to decide on a case. The terminology of source of law contains different meaning. It can be seen from historical, sociological, philosophical, and scientific perspective of law. Each discipline construes it from their perspective with regard to law. Historians, sociologists, philosophers, and jurists see law from their point of view. For a historian and a sociologist, a law is not more than social symptom and should be scientifically

35. *Ibid.*, p. 48.
36. *Ibid.*, pp. 48–49.
37. Prof. Mr Dr L.J. van Apeldoorn, *Pengantar Ilmu Hukum*, p. 41 (PT Pradnya Paramita 1996).
38. *Ibid.*, p. 41.

approached. Philosopher and jurist, in contrast, see the law as a set of conduct and value system.[39]

42. Prof. Dr Achmad Sanusi, S.H. divides sources of formal law as follows:[40]

(1) Law.
(2) Agreement.
(3) Treaty.
(4) Customs.
(5) Jurisprudence.
(6) Doctrine.

Drs C.S.T Kansil, S.H. divides sources of formal law as follows:

(1) Law.
(2) Custom.
(3) Jurisprudence.
(4) Treaty.
(5) Doctrine.

Prof. Mr Dr L. J. Van Apeldoorn divides sources of formal law as follows:

(1) Law.
(2) Customs.
(3) Treaty.

43. Despite differences legal experts' opinion, the writer divides and discusses each of the following sources of law:

(1) Law

Law is a regulation made by the House of Representatives with a joint approval by the President.[41] A law has the same rank with the Government Regulation in lieu of Law that can be promulgated by the President in emergency.[42]

(2) Jurisprudence

As a legal formal source, it is highly related to the judge's duty. Jurisprudence is a previous decision that is often followed and used as a ground of decision by the judge on the same matter. It is used by the judge in giving the decision on a dispute that has not been regulated by the regulations.

---

39. Prof. Dr Peter Mahmud Marzuki, S.H., M.S., LL.M, *Pengantar Ilmu Hukum*, p. 255 (revised edition. Prenadamedia Group 2013).
40. Amiruddin Pabbu, S.H., M.H., and Rahman Syamsuddin S.H., M.H., *Pengantar Ilmu Hukum*, p. 57 (1st edition. Mitra Wacana Media 2014).
41. Article 1 Number 3 of Law Number 12 of 2011 on Formation of Laws and Regulations.
42. Article 7 of Law Number 12 of 2011 on Formation of Laws and Regulations.

(3) Customs

Customs can be a source of law when it has become a definite behaviour. If a society already has the awareness of a certain behaviour or even convinced that it is an obligation, then that circumstance is an inseparable complementary requirement. Customs definition is very broad, since customary law is not written.

(4) Treaty

A treaty is an agreement under international law entered into by actors in international law, namely sovereign states and international organizations. A treaty may also be known as an (international) agreement, protocol, covenant, convention, pact, or exchange of letters, among other terms. Regardless of terminology, all of these forms of agreements are, under international law, equally considered treaties and the rules are the same.[43]

(5) Doctrine

The doctrine has an important position as a source of law, especially in the international sphere. International Court of Justice in its Statute admits that in considering and deciding a dispute, various guides can be used, including, international conventions, international customs, the general principles of law recognized by civilized nations, judicial decisions, and legal doctrine.

§3. Introduction to the Law of Property and Trust

I. Historical Origins and Evolution

44. A property law is a law governing how to increase a person's asset, what properties are, and how to defend their properties from other parties.

45. In a legal science, a property law is part of closed law, meaning that any person cannot deviate from it. The provisions are absolute and unchallenged, unless it is allowed under the laws.

46. The closed nature of property law means that a person cannot waive any of its provisions governed by the laws in accordance with their agreement. Therefore, any provisions set out by the laws as property and which include all of its rights cannot be challenged, waived by or based on agreement by definite persons, or any person cannot, by virtue of his own interest, create a new property outside what is determined under the laws.[44]

43. Treaty. https://en.wikipedia.org/wiki/Treaty.
44. Kartini Mulyadi and Gunawan Widjaya, *Kebendaan pada Umumnya*, p. 16 (1st edition. Kencana 2003).

47. Property law is not only governed by ICC. Since the promulgation of Law Number 5 of 1960 on Principle Provisions of Agrarian ('Agrarian Law'), some provisions of Chapter II of ICC are no longer applicable.

48. On the decision section of the Agrarian Law, it states that it revokes Chapter II of ICC to the extent on the provisions on earth, water, and natural resources contained in it, unless provisions on hypothec that are still applicable on the commencement of the law.

49. With the promulgation of Agrarian Law and revocation of Chapter II of ICC related to earth, water, and natural resources, Sri Soedewi Masjchoen Sofwan in *Hukum Perdata: Hukum Benda* states as follows:

(1) Clauses that are fully applicable:

(a) Clauses on movable goods, Articles 505, 509–518 of ICC;
(b) Clauses on delivery of movable goods, Articles 612, 826, 827 of ICC;
(c) Clauses on inheritance, Articles 830–1130 of ICC;
(d) Clauses on preferred receivables, Articles 1131–1149 of ICC;
(e) Clauses on pledge, since pledge is only applicable to movable goods, Articles 1156–1150 of ICC;
(f) Clauses on hypothec, since hypothec is exempted by the Agrarian Law, except for clauses that are not applicable under Article 31 OV Stb. 1848 Number 10.[45]

(2) Clauses that are no longer applicable:

(a) Clauses on immovable goods that are only related to rights of land;
(b) Clauses on means to obtain ownership only related to land;
(c) Clauses on delivery of immovable goods never applied;
(d) Clauses on sweatshop, Article 673 of ICC;
(e) Clauses on rights and obligations of owners of neighbouring lands, Articles 625–672 of ICC;
(f) Clauses on land servitude (*erfdienstbaarheid*), Articles 674–710 of ICC;
(g) Clauses on Opstal right, Articles 711–719 of ICC;
(h) Clauses on Erfpacht, Articles 720–736 of ICC;
(i) Clauses on land interest and tithing, Articles 737–755 of ICC.

(3) Clauses that are still applicable but not absolute, where they are no longer applicable related to earth, water, and natural resources contained in it, and are still applicable for other goods:

(a) Clauses on goods in general;
(b) Clauses on how to differentiate goods, Articles 503–505 of ICC;
(c) Clauses on goods not related to land, between Articles 529–568 of ICC;
(d) Clauses on ownership right not related to land, Article 570 of ICC;

45. After the promulgation of Law Number 4 of 1996 on Mortgage, the clauses on hypothec are no longer applicable since they are revoked by the Mortgage Law.

(e) Clauses on rights to levy result (*vruchtgebruik*) to the extent not related to land, Article 756 of ICC;
(f) Clauses on usage rights to the extent not related to land, Article 818 of ICC.

50. As a follow up of Agrarian Law, in 1996, a Law Number 4 of 1996 on Mortgage was promulgated. Three years later, Law Number 42 of 1999 on Fiduciary Security ('Fiduciary Security Law') was also promulgated. Mortgage Law governs security for immovable goods, whereas Fiduciary Security Law governs security for movable goods, which was previously regulated under the jurisprudences.

II. The Concept of Ownership

A. Unity and Fragmentation

51. Article 1296 of ICC regulates that an agreement is able to be divided or undivided as far as such agreement concerns about a certain good which its delivery or the execution thereof can be divided or undivided either obviously or in calculation.

52. A divided good means a good which by its nature can be divided without damaging or causing problems in using or enjoying it, or losing its function. Examples are delivery of rice, money, sand.[46]

53. An undivided good means a good which by its nature is undivided without damaging it or causing problems in using or enjoying it, or losing its function. Examples are delivery of a horse, a table, a car.

54. ICC may regulate that a good which can be divided, by its nature, to be altered as undivided.[47] This is regulated under Article 1297 of ICC which states that an agreement is undivided, although the involved object or the execution thereof by its nature can be divided, if the good or the action, according to the purpose of the agreement cannot be delivered or performed partially. Examples are a payment of debt, in a certain amount as determined on a certain time.[48]

B. Immovable and Real Property (see also Part I)

55. Every property is tangible or intangible;[49] every property is movable or immovable.[50] Every movable property is consumable or not exhausted; property is consumable, if by consuming it becomes exhausted.[51]

56. Article 506 of ICC provides the following definitions on immovable properties:

(1) Curtilages and anything built on it.

---

46. Kartini Mulyadi and Gunawan Widjaya, *Kebendaan pada Umumnya*, p. 46 (1st edition. Kencana 2003).
47. *Ibid.*, p. 47.
48. *Ibid.*, p. 47.
49. Article 503 of ICC.
50. Article 504 of ICC.
51. Article 505 of ICC.

(2) Mills, except for mills installed to the boat.
(3) Trees and farms' plant, which roots stuck to the ground; unplugged fruits, and so does the minerals such as coal, burned, trash as long as those things have not been separated and dug from the ground.
(4) Cut-down wood from the woods and wood from the high trees, as long as those wood have not been cut.
(5) Water pipes and drainage from the house and curtilage; and in general anything rooted to the curtilage or nailed to the building of the house.

57. Further, Article 507 of ICC provides meaning over immovable properties with regards to their use:

(1) In the factory: the products of the factory itself, millers, hardener, iron and such kinds of immovable property, iron-presser/flanker, steamer-pot, fireplace, big pots, barrels and other tools which are included in the principal of a factory, although such things are not embedded or nailed.
(2) In the housing: mirrors, paintings, and other accessories, as long as such things are vested to the board or stones which is part of the wall, fence or the hall plaster, as long as such things are not nailed.
(3) In the ownership of land: manure-pool or pile of fat provided for fertilizing the soil; dove included in the group, eatable bird-nest, as long as such has not been plucked; fish in the pond.
(4) Building materials from the building demolition; if provided for rebuilding such building; and in general; goods which by the owner are connected to the immovable corporeal to be used forever.
The owner is deemed to connect such things as the immovable property, if those things are attached to the works of digging, carpeting, or stone-paving, or if such things cannot be loosened without breaking or damaging the parts of such immovable property, where the goods are attached to.

58. Some rights are considered as immovable property, namely:[52]

(1) Right to use the outcome and right to use upon the immovable property.
(2) Right of land servitude.
(3) Right of joint-estate.
(4) Right to cultivate.
(5) Land interest, either in the form of cash or in the form of property.
(6) Tithing.
(7) Market-tax, which is recognized by the government and special rights, which are attached to it.
(8) Complaint to claim for the surrender or reverting of the immovable property.

59. Right of land servitude, right of joint-estate, right to cultivate, land interest, and tithing are no longer applicable since the promulgation of Agrarian Law.

60. Article 16 of Agrarian Law provides various type of rights of land, namely:

52. Article 508 of ICC.

(1) Right of ownership.
(2) Right to cultivate.
(3) Right to build.
(4) Right of use.
(5) Right of lease.
(6) Right to open land.
(7) Right to collect forest' production.
(8) Other rights excluded from the above rights that will be determined under the law and temporary rights.

61. Right of ownership is inherited, the strongest and the fullest that can be owned by a person over land, on the condition that it has a social function.[53] Only an Indonesian can own right of ownership.[54]

62. Right to cultivate is a right to cultivate land directly controlled by the state, for a period of twenty-five or thirty-five years, for farm, fishery, or animal husbandry.[55] This right is granted for a land of at least 5 hectares. Right to cultivate can be owned by an Indonesian or legal entity established under Indonesian law and domiciled in Indonesia.[56]

63. Right to build is a right to construct and own buildings over land not self-owned, for a period of thirty years.[57] This right can be owned by an Indonesian or legal entity established under Indonesian law and domiciled in Indonesia.[58]

64. Right of use is a right to use and/or collect land's production directly controlled by the state or other people's land, having the authority and obligation as determined in the granting decision by the official or within the agreement with the landowner, that is not a lease agreement or land cultivation agreement, all things that are not contrary to the soul and provisions of Agrarian Law. This right can be granted for a certain period or as long as it is used for a specific purpose; for free, with a payment or any type of services.[59] This right can be owned by Indonesian, foreigner domiciled in Indonesia, legal entity established under Indonesian law and domiciled in Indonesia, foreign legal entity having its representative office in Indonesia.[60]

65. Right of lease over building is not clearly defined under Agrarian Law. This right is used if a person would like to use other person's land for building, by paying rent.[61] Holders of this right are Indonesians, foreigners domiciled in Indonesia, a legal entity established under Indonesian law and domiciled in Indonesia, and a foreign legal entity having its representative office in Indonesia.[62]

---

53. Article 20 of Agrarian Law.
54. Article 21 para. (1) of Agrarian Law.
55. Article 28 para.s (1) and (2) of Agrarian Law.
56. Article 30 of Agrarian Law.
57. Article 35 para. (1) of Agrarian Law.
58. Article 36 para. (1) of Agrarian Law.
59. Article 41 paras (1) and (2) of Agrarian Law.
60. Article 41 of Agrarian Law.
61. Article 44 para. (1) of Agrarian Law.
62. Article 45 of Agrarian Law.

66. Right to open land and to collect forest's production can only be owned by an Indonesian and determined by government regulation. By having the right to legally collect forest's production, it does not mean that the ownership of land is owned.[63]

C. *Movable and Personal Property (see also Part II)*

67. Movable property differs by its character: can be moved such as table, chair, or can move by itself such as animals. Ships and boats and all things installed on it are movable goods.

68. Movable property is determined by law, i.e. right over movable goods, such as right to collect yield over movable goods, right of use over movable goods, agreements and claims concerning the amount of money which can be claimed or which concerns to the movable property.

69. Any person, who possesses movable property that is not in the form of an interest or receivable that is not payable to the bearer, is deemed as lawful owner.[64]

III. Estate and Patrimony

A. *Unity and Fragmentation*

70. In Indonesia, there are many different estate systems applicable to Indonesian nationals. One of the examples is Article 136 *Wet op de Staats Inrichting van Nederland Indische*, abbreviated as *Indische Staatsregeling* or IS of 1925, effective since 1 January 1926.[65]

71. Article 136 of IS derives from Article 109 *Reglement op get belied der Regeerings van Nederland Indische*, abbreviated as *Regeering Reglement* (RR Staatsblad dated 1 January 1854 Number 29 jo. *Staatsblad* Dutch East Indies of 1855 Number 2) applicable since 1 January 1855 which at the beginning comes from Articles 6–10 AB (*Algemeene Bepalingen van Wetgeving*) of 1848. This regulation stipulates three group of Dutch East Indies, as follows:

(1) European, i.e. Dutch, Germany, British, French, including Japan, United States, Australia and Canada.
(2) Foreign East, i.e. Chinese, Arab, India, Pakistan, Muangthai, and others.
(3) Indigenous, i.e. Indonesian comprising of 19 *Kukuban* law according to Prof. Van Vollenhoven and BZN Ter Haar.[66]

72. The applicable law for the above-mentioned groups is regulated under Article 131 *Indische Staatsregeling* as promulgated through *Staatsblad* 1919 Number 286 and *Staatsblad* Dutch East Indies of 1919 Number 621.[67]

63. Article 47 of Agrarian Law.
64. Article 1977 para. (1) of ICC.
65. Maman Suparman, *Hukum Waris Perdata*, p. 1 (1st edition. Sinar Grafika 2015).
66. Maman Suparman, *Hukum Waris Perdata*, p. 1 (1st edition. Sinar Grafika 2015).
67. *Ibid.*, p. 2.

73. For European, the civil law, i.e., BW and commercial law, i.e., WvK are applicable in accordance with the concordance principle. For Foreign East, their own customary law is applicable under Article 75 RR, *Staatsblad* 1854 Number 129 in Netherlands jo. *Staatsbland* Dutch East Indies of 1855 Number 2. For Indigenous, religion laws, people's assembly, customs or *Godsdiestige Wetten, Volkinsteling en Grebruiken* or customary law.[68]

74. Inheritance occurs only due to death.[69] The heirs by law assume possession of the properties, rights, and receivables of the deceased. In the event of a dispute over who shall be the heir, and who shall be authorized to hold title to the property, the judge may order that the properties shall be held in the court's safekeeping. The State should endeavour to be placed as possessor by the judge, and shall be obligated to seal the estate, and have an estate description drafted in the form of an acceptance of inheritances stipulated pursuant to the privilege of estate description; failure to do so renders the State liable for compensation of costs, damages, and interest.[70]

75. An undivided estate does not have to remain undivided. Division of the estate may, notwithstanding any conflicting prohibition, be demanded at any time. It may, however, be agreed not to carry out the estate division during a specific period of time. Such agreement shall be binding for five years only, but may be extended upon expiration of each term.[71]

76. The creditors of the testator, including the legatees, shall be entitled to oppose the estate division. The deed of the estate division, drawn up after such opposition and prior to compliance with that which was due and collectable during the opposition, for the benefit of the creditor or legatee, shall be void with regard to such creditor or legatee.

77. In the event that the heirs have free use of their properties and are in attendance, the estate division takes place in such manner and pursuant to such deed as they deem appropriate.

B. Trust and Fiduciary Mechanisms (see also Parts IV and V)

78. The properties which an individual leaves upon his demise belong to his legal heirs, to the extent that he has not legally disposed of the same by will.[72] A testament or last will is a deed, containing a statement of an individual's wishes and intents to take effect following his death, and which can be revoked by him/her.[73]

79. A testator may, by last will, or by private deed, or by specific notarial deed, appoint one or more executors of his last will. He may also nominate several individuals to succeed one another in the event of unavailability.[74]

80. The executors of testament must prepare an estate description of the properties in the inheritance, in the presence of the heirs following the proper summons of those

68. *Ibid.*, pp. 2–3.
69. Article 830 of ICC.
70. Article 833 of ICC.
71. Article 1066 of ICC.
72. Article 874 of ICC.
73. Article 875 of ICC.
74. Article 1005 of ICC.

who reside within Indonesia.[75] They have to ensure that the last will of the deceased shall be implemented, and in the event of dispute, they can appear in court to maintain the validity of the last will.[76]

81. The testator may, by last will or by specific notarial deed, appoint one or more managers to manage the properties left to his heirs or legatees, during their lives or for a specific period of time, provided that it does not interfere with the unobstructed vesting of the legal share of the heirs.[77]

82. The executors of last wills, including the managers, may be discharged for the same reasons applicable for the discharge of guardians as stipulated in the ICC.

IV. Possession and Title

83. Possession is interpreted as the holding or enjoyment of properties, which an individual, either in person or through another person, has within his power, as if he has actual title thereto.[78]

84. To have a possession status, a person must act as if he is the owner of the property in his possession. This means that the legal relationship of a person having the possession over the property is a direct relationship between legal subject (person) and legal object (property) resulting in the property law that gives rights to the possessor a property right to defend it from third party and to enjoy, use, and utilize it for the benefit of the possessor.[79]

85. Possession may be either in good faith or in bad faith.[80] Possession is in good faith, if at the time the owner acquired the properties he was unaware of the defects therein.[81] Possession is in bad faith, if the owner is aware that the properties in his possession are not his property. The owner considered to possess in bad faith from the time that a lawsuit is filed against him, in the event that the judgment pursuant to the lawsuit is against him.[82] The good faith of the owner is always presumed; the onus of proof of bad faith is on the individual who alleges bad faith.[83]

86. Properties which cannot be traded commercially cannot be an object of possession.[84] This is a logical consequence of legal relationship in property law. A possessed good must have economical value that is tradable, not a good that belongs to a state of public interest, is an essential requirement so that the property can increase the asset of a person positively (property law speaks about increase of a person's asset

75. Article 1010 of ICC.
76. Article 1011 of ICC.
77. Article 1019 of ICC.
78. Article 529 of ICC.
79. Kartini Muljadi and Gunawan Widjaja, *Kedudukan Berkuasa dan Hak Milik*, p. 14 (1st edition. Kencana 2004).
80. Article 530 of ICC.
81. Article 531 of ICC.
82. Article 532 of ICC.
83. Article 533 of ICC.
84. Article 537 of ICC.

positively, i.e., different than a law on agreement that speaks about obligation according to Article 1131 of ICC[85] which represents a negative aspect of a person's asset).[86]

87. Ownership is the right to have free enjoyment of property and to dispose thereof absolutely, provided that an individual does not violate the laws of the public ordinances stipulated by those who have been granted authority to do so, in the course of using such properties, and provided that an individual does not interfere with other individual's rights; the aforementioned shall be without prejudice to expropriation in the public interest subject to the individual's right to appropriate compensation, pursuant to the legal regulations.[87]

88. By possessing a property according to ownership right, a person holding the title is authorized to possess it peacefully and to defend it against any party intending to disturb his peacefulness while he possesses, uses, and utilizes the property.[88]

89. Ownership of properties cannot be acquired in any manner other than by appropriation, attachment, prescription, legal or testamentary succession, and by assignment or delivery pursuant to a transfer of legal title, originating from the individual who was entitled to dispose of the property.[89]

---

85. All movable and immovable properties of the debtor, either present or future, serve as securities for the personal obligations of the debtor.
86. Kartini Muljadi and Gunawan Widjaja, *Kedudukan Berkuasa dan Hak Milik*, pp. 20–21 (1st edition. Kencana 2004).
87. Article 570 of ICC.
88. *Ibid.*, pp. 131–132.
89. Article 584 of ICC.

Part I. Immovable Property and Real Property

Chapter 1. General Classification

90. There are three classifications of immovable property based on ICC, namely:

(1) A property which is immovable, and is divided into (a) land, (b) anything attached to the land, grown, rooted and branched such as plants, fruits that have not been reaped, and (c) all things anything which is attached to the soil or permanently fixed on a plot of land or to a building.

(2) A property intended to be integrated since it is repeatedly used with the immovable property such as (a) all machines, kettles, and any other equipment intended to be used to run a factory (b) in residences, all mirrors, paintings, and other accessories attached as part of the building (c) in a plantation, the dunghill designated for the fertilization of the land; the pigeons belonging to a flock of pigeons; the edible birds' nests, to the extent that they have not been collected; the fish in the rivers (d) building materials resulting from the demolition of the building, if they are designated to be used to re-build the building.

(3) Several rights over immovable properties mentioned above, such as (a) the use of the proceeds from and use of the immovable properties; (b) servitude; (c) the right to have buildings, structures, or plants on another person's property (*opstal*); (d) the hereditary right of a tenant to occupy a piece of land; (e) ground rent, either due in the form of money or in kind; (f) the one-tenth right; (g) the bazaars or markets, acknowledged by the government, and the privileges relevant thereto; (h) the lawsuits, filed to reclaim immovable properties or deliver them.

91. Since the three classifications above is revoked by Agrarian Law, there is essentially no classifications of immovable properties, other than rights of land stipulated under Agrarian Law and Indonesian ships, with a gross volume of at least twenty cubic metres.[90]

90. Article 314 of Indonesia Commercial Code.

92. It is the obligation by the government to implement land registration throughout the whole territory of the Republic of Indonesia in order to guarantee legal certainty. The registration includes: (1) surveying, mapping, and recording of land in a book; (2) registration of rights of land and their transfer; and (3) granting documentary instruments of evidence of right, which shall serve as a strong instrument of evidence.[91] Certificate of land will be evidence that the land has been registered.

93. A certificate of land is a right-evidencing document which serves as strong evidence of the physical data and juridical data shown in it as long as these physical and juridical data match what is shown in the relevant survey document (*surat ukur*) and book of land (*buku tanah*). If a land parcel for which a certificate has been legally issued on behalf of a certain individual or a corporate body that has acquired the land parcel in question in good faith and has in reality been possessing it, any other parties which think they have rights thereon can no longer claim for these rights in the case where, within five years following the issuance of the said certificate, they never raised their objections in writing to the holder of the certificate and to the Head of the relevant land office and never filed a lawsuit with the court over the possession of the land parcel in question or the issuance of the certificate.[92]

94. By having a certificate of land, one is considered as having a strong instrument of evidence that one legally owns the land, even though that instrument is not absolute evidence. Nevertheless, the prevailing regulation also stipulates that no other party can have a claim over the land five years after the issuance of certificate of land,.

91. Article 19 of Agrarian Law.
92. Article 32 of Land Registration Reg.

Chapter 3. Equitable Interests

95. Since the promulgation of Agrarian Law, all types of land in Indonesia are converted into right of land as stipulated under the Agrarian Law. The period between 1960 to date is more than fifty years. But due to various reasons and non-completion of systematic land registration programmes in Indonesia, one can find that many rights of land have not been registered or certificated. Therefore, the government issued a government regulation Number 24 of 1997 on Land Registration ('Land Registration Reg') to provide opportunities for the people having rights of land prior to promulgation of Agrarian Law that have not been registered under Land Registration Regulation.

96. For those who have right of land deriving from the conversion of an old right prior to promulgation of Agrarian Law is proven with evidence in the form of written documents, witnesses' information,[93] and/or statement made by the party in question which will be evaluated by the relevant officials for its adequate content of truth to register their rights, of the right holder, and of other parties' right which encumber it.[94] If the old right of land has been transferred to other party, the written document shall also include the evidence of transfer of right.[95]

97. If there is no evidence available to register their old right prior to promulgation of Agrarian Law, the land registration can be carried out on the basis of the fact that the land parcel has been physically possessed for twenty consecutive years or more by the person applying for land registration and his/her predecessors, provided that: (1) the possession of land parcel has been made in good faith and in a transparent way by the person applying for land registration and (2) the possession of land parcel was not questioned by the relevant customary law community or the relevant village/sub-district community or other parties, before or during the period of two-month announcement as stipulated under the Land Registration Reg.[96]

98. Elucidation of Article 24 paragraph (1) provides the types of written evidence to apply for land registration:

(1) original copy of the *akte hak eigendom* (deed on right of ownership) which was issued based on *Overschrijvings Ordonnantie* (Conveyance Ordinance) [S.1834-27] with a note on it that the right of *eigendom* has been converted into *Hak Milik* (right of ownership); or
(2) a *Hak Milik* (right of Ownership) document which was issued under the applicable regulations of the relevant Kingdom/Sultanate; or
(3) a *Hak Milik* certificate which has been issued under Regulation of the Minister of Agrarian Affairs Number 9 of 1959; or
(4) a *Hak Milik* (right of ownership) granting decree issued by an authorized official, either before or after the enactment of the UUPA, which does not require the

93. Elucidation of the article explains that a witness means a person who is good at giving a testimony and who is knowledgeable of the history of ownership of the land parcel in question.
94. Article 24 para. (1) of Land Registration Reg.
95. Elucidation of Art. 24 para. (1) of Land Registration Reg.
96. Article 24 para. (2) of Land Registration Reg.

holder to have his land to be registered but mentions other obligations for the holder, all of which have been fulfilled by the holder; or

(5) a right-transfer deed made in private prior to the enactment of Land Registration Reg and signed by the Adat Chief/Village Chief/Kelurahan Head; or
(6) a right-transfer deed made by the PPAT, of which the land parcel in question has not been recorded in the *buku tanah*; or
(7) a *Wakaf* (Edification) Promise Deed/*Wakaf* Promise Letter which was made either before or after the enactment of Government Regulation Number 28 of 1977; or
(8) an auction report made by the relevant auction official; or
(9) a document on the designating or purchase of a land parcel as a replacement for the land acquired by the government/local administration; or
(10) a land tax receipt (*Petuk Pajak Bumi, Landrente, girik, pipil, or ketitir*) or Verponding Indonesia issued prior to the enactment of Government Regulation Number 10 of 1961; or
(11) a land history certificate made by *Kantor Pelayanan Pajak Bumi and Bangunan* (the Land and Building Taxation Office); or
(12) other written evidence by whatever names as meant in the Articles II, VI, and VII of the UUPA regarding provisions concerning Conversion.

99. Elucidation of Article 24 paragraph (2) of Land Regulation Reg also stipulates further requirements for the registering of a land right where there is no evidence in writing at all, namely:

(1) that the possession and use of the land parcel in question have been taking place in reality and good faith for at least twenty consecutive years;
(2) that the possession and use of the land parcel in question have never been claimed against and, hence, can be regarded as having been recognized and vindicated by the relevant customary law community or by the members of the relevant village/sub-district office;
(3) that the truth mentioned in points (1) and (2) above is strengthened by testimonies from trustworthy people;
(4) that the opportunities have been provided through the two-month period of announcement for other parties to raise objections;
(5) that the things mentioned above have been scrutinized for truth;
(6) that the conclusions concerning the status of the land parcel in question and the right holder have been made and presented in the form of a decision on recognizing the right in question by the land office's officials.

100. Indonesian Agrarian Law does not recognize expiry principle that is stipulated under ICC.[97] Under Supreme Court decision Number 187 K/SIP/1956 dated 10 January 1957, it is clear that customary law, which is the legal basis of agrarian law in Indonesia, does not have any expiry period.

97. Under Art. 1967 of ICC it is stipulated that all legal claims, either with property or personal character, terminates due to expiry of thirty year time, whereas the person designating that expiry, does not have to show a legal title, and against him no exception can be made which is based on bad faith.

Chapter 4. Limited Interests

§1. Usufruct

101. Agrarian Law does not have a 'usufruct' concept. But there is a similar concept of usufruct, namely right of use (*hak pakai*). Under Agrarian Law, right of use means the right to use and/or take the product of the land which is directly controlled by State or other landowner, which authorities and duties are specified in the decree granting rights (State land) or in the agreement with the landowner which is not a lease agreement or land cultivation agreement.

102. It can be concluded that the right of use is the right which can be obtained on agricultural or non-agricultural land. The word 'use' indicates that the land can be used for non-agriculture purpose. The word 'harvest' indicates that the land can be used for agricultural purpose as factors of production.[98]

§2. Building and Planting Rights

103. Building and planting rights are similar to right to build (*hak guna bangunan*), right to cultivate (*hak guna usaha*), and right of use (*hak pakai*) as set forth in Agrarian Law. While right to build means right to construct/build and own a building on land that is not owned by the holder of the right within a certain period, and right to cultivate means to use or cultivate the land which are directly controlled by the State during a certain period for agriculture, fishery, plantation, and animal husbandry, and only right of use is able to be used for either agricultural or non-agricultural purpose.

§3. Leasehold Interests: Chattels Real (see also Part II)

104. Leasehold interests are similar to right of lease for building (*hak sewa untuk bangunan*) under Agrarian Law. It means a right of lease over land, where the lessee is authorized to use other party's land for building purpose, by paying to the landlord a definite amount of rent.[99]

§4. Emphyteusis and Rent Charge

105. Emphyteusis is not regulated under Agrarian Law. It is however a common practice in Indonesia, especially between governmental institutions and private parties.

98. Prof. Arie S. Hutagalung, S.H., M.LI., *The Principles of Indonesian Agrarian Law*, p. 52 (2nd edition. Badan Penerbit FHUI 2015).
99. Article 44 para. (1) of Agrarian Law.

106. It is normally called as build, operate, and transfer (BOT) agreement or build, transfer, and operate (BTO) agreement. Government Regulation Number 27 of 2014 on Management of State/Regional-owned Goods ('GR 27/2014') defines BOT as the utilization of State/Regional-owned goods in the form of land by other party by constructing building and/or its facilities, utilized by the other party for a definite agreed period, of which land and building and/or their facilities and infrastructures are returned after the lapse of its period.[100]Whereas, BTO is defined as the utilization of State/Regional-owned goods in the form of land by other party by constructing building and/or its facilities, and after the construction is completed to be delivered and used by that other party within a definite agreed period.[101]

§5. Use and Habitation/Occupation

107. A similar right to use and habitation is a right of lodging as stipulated under Agrarian Law. Right of lodging means a right that authorizes a person to construct and occupy a house on garden land of others (*numpang sari/magersari*). Right of lodging is essentially a type of right of use species, but its legal relationship is weak, easily expropriated by the owner of garden since there is no payment required (gratis).[102]

§6. Easements and Profits

108. There is no concept of easements and profits under Agrarian Law. We can however find a similar concept through its implementing regulation. If right to cultivate, right to build, or right of use, due to geographical circumstance or environment or any other causes, its location confines or closes the yard or other plot of land from public road or water channel, those holders of right of land is obligated to provide the way out or water channel or other easements for that confined yard or plot of land.[103]

§7. Licences

109. There is no concept of licence in Agrarian Law. But there is a similar concept, namely a granting of right to build or right of use over right of ownership or right of management (*hak pengelolaan*). Agrarian Law provides possibilities for two parties to enter into an agreement, where the original landlord (owner of right of ownership or holder of right of management) will grant a right to build or right of use, for a definite period of time, to be used by the applicant or investor, during that period.

---

100. Article 1 point 14 of GR 27/2014.
101. Article 1 point 15 of GR 27/2014.
102. Prof. Arie S. Hutagalung, S.H., M.LI., *The Principles of Indonesian Agrarian Law*, p. 62 (2nd editrion. Badan Penerbit FHUI 2015).
103. Articles 13, 31 and 51 of Government Regulation Number 40 of 1996 on Right to Cultivate, Right to Build, and Right of Use of Land.

110. The application of the above-mentioned concept will involve the formation and execution of a standardized form made before the Land Conveyancing Officer (*Pejabat Pembuat Akta Tanah – PPAT*). This deed will then be registered at land office. The land office will afterward issue a certificate of land according to the agreement between the parties. The period of the certificate of land will depend on the type of right of land whether it is a right to build or right of use.

111. The holder of right to build or right of use over right of ownership or right of management can use the land during the period, sell, and/or pledge it subject to approval by the original landlord granting that particular land right.

§8. Restrictive Covenants

112. Restrictive covenants are applicable under the prevailing laws and regulations or made by the parties through an agreement. Agrarian Law stipulates that it is a duty of every individual, corporation, or institution which has a legal relationship with land to take care of the land, to improve its fertility, and to prevent it from damage by taking into consideration the interest of the economically weak.[104] Violation of this provision shall be punished with imprisonment of not more than three months and/or with a fine of at most Rp 10,000.[105]

113. Under Law Number 28 of 2002 on Building ('Building Law'), it is stipulated that the requirements for building comfort includes movement space, inter-room relation, air condition in a room, view, and vibration level as well as noise level. View comfort is a condition where the person's private right in doing his activities in the building is not disrupted from other surrounding buildings.[106]

104. Article 15 of Agrarian Law.
105. Article 52 para. (1) of Agrarian Law.
106. Article 26 para. (5) of Building Law.

Chapter 5. Security Interests (see also Parts II, IV, and V)

114. The security for the land is regulated under Mortgage Law. After waiting for around thirty-four years since the promulgation of Agrarian Law, Mortgage Law was promulgated on 9 April 1996. This law essentially is intended as a replacement of hypothec regulated under ICC, where its applicability was temporary until the promulgation of Mortgage Law.

115. The general elucidation of Mortgage Law already mentions that a strong security institution is made available by Agrarian Law that can be pledged over land, namely mortgage, as a replacement of hypothec and *credietverband.* For over thirty years since Agrarian Law became effective, the mortgage institution is not functioning as it was intended for, as stipulated by Article 51 of Agrarian Law. For that period, as stipulated under the transition clause, hypothec provisions under ICC and *credietverband* provisions as set forth in Staatsblad 1908-542 as amended by Staatsblad 1937-190, so long as has not been regulated otherwise by Agrarian Law, are still applicable.[107]

116. Mortgage right over land including goods related to land is defined as security right pledged over right of land as set forth in Agrarian Law, including or excluding other goods that are integrated with the land, for a specific payment of debt that gives a preferential right to a certain creditor against other creditors.[108]

117. Right of lands that are able to be mortgaged are right of ownership, right to cultivate, right to build over state land, right of management or right of ownership, right of use over state land and ownership.[109] There are two essential conditions mentioned in its elucidation, namely, the right of land must be registered and mortgage must be recorded in the book of land and certificate of land so that the public may know about the legal status of the land (publication). Second, the right of land must have inherent nature that it is transferable, so that if required it can be executed to repay the secured debt.

118. A building that cannot be mortgaged is able to be secured through a fiduciary security. Fiduciary Security Law defines fiduciary security as a security right over movable goods, tangible or intangible, and immovable goods particularly building that cannot be mortgaged, that is controlled by the debtor, as security over payment of certain debt that gives preferential position to the creditor against the other creditors.[110]

119. Even though hypothec provisions are applicable to immovable goods, some exceptions apply. Indonesian ships, with a gross volume of at least twenty cubic metres, may be entered into a shipping register in line with the regulations which shall be stated by separate ordinance.[111] Ships recorded in the shipping register, ships under construction, and shares in such ships and ships under construction may be mortgaged (hypothec).[112]

107. Chapter I, para. (2) of General elucidation of Mortgage Law.
108. Article 1 point 1 of Mortgage Law.
109. Article 4 paras (1) and (2) of Mortgage Law.
110. Article 1 point 2 of Fiducia Law.
111. Article 314 para. (1) of Indonesian Commercial Code.
112. Article 314 para. (3) of Indonesian Commercial Code.

120. Under Article 314 paragraphs (1) and (3) of Indonesian Commercial Code, registered ships in the shipping register are classified as registered movable goods or can be deemed as immovable goods since those ships can be mortgaged (through hypothec). Nevertheless, only ships with a volume of at least twenty cubic metres can be mortgaged.[113]

121. Registration over ships having volume less than 20 cubic metre is not possible since the purpose of ship registration is to obtain ship's nationality. Therefore, registered ships are compared with immovable goods. For ships less than 20 cubic metre, they can be pledged or secured through a fiduciary security.[114]

122. The same application is applied for aircraft and helicopter. Under civil law, aircraft's legal status is considered as immovable goods. This relates to the granting of status according to civil law's classification, especially on property that is still embraced by majority of the states in the world. This affects over regulation of civil law that controls aircraft as an object, among others, can have a direct relationship with the security institution particularly hypothec.[115]

123. Aircraft and helicopter that obtain registration mark and Indonesian nationality can be mortgaged (through hypothec). Law Number 15 of 1992 ('Flight Law') stipulates that its hypothec must be registered.[116] Hypothec provisions applicable for aircraft and helicopter are provisions under ICC, provided that it does not hinder other encumbrance according to the prevailing laws.[117]

113. Rachmadi Usman, S.H., M.H., *Hukum Jaminan Keperdataan*, p. 291 (1st edition. Sinar Grafika 2008).
114. *Ibid.*, p. 291.
115. *Ibid.*, p. 306.
116. Article 12 of Flight Law.
117. Elucidation of Art. 12 of Flight Law.

Chapter 6. Joint Ownership

§1. Joint Ownership of Immovable Property

I. In General

124. Joint ownership can be applied over a right of land and a joint land in a condominium. Deriving from the state's controlling right over land, there are different types of right over land surface, called as land that can be granted to and owned by individuals, individually or jointly with other people and legal entities.[118] This fundamental provision of Agrarian Law is further implemented under a government regulation.

125. If a right of land or a right of ownership over condominium unit is jointly owned by a number of individuals or corporate bodies, one certificate may be issued and delivered to one of the joint right holders who has been appointed in writing by all other joint right holders.[119] It is also possible to issue and deliver the certificate to each joint right holder containing name and portion of each of that joint right.[120]

II. Co-ownership Applied to Apartment Buildings

126. Ownership over joint right of land for a condominium is regulated under Law Number 20 of 2011 on Condominium ('Condominium Law'). A certificate of right of ownership over condominium unit is defined as an evidence of ownership over condominium unit with the right of ownership, right to build, or right of use over state land, as well as right to build or right of use over right of management.[121] This certificate consists of copy of book of land and measurement letter over right of joint land, floor layout of the condominium showing the owned unit, and title of division depicting portion of joint right over joint facility, joint equipment, and joint land.[122]

127. The joint ownership in a condominium or apartment buildings covers ownership over joint facility, joint equipment, and joint land. A joint land is defined as a piece of land right or leased land for building that is used on a jointly basis, inseparably, where a condominium is built over it and its boundaries are determined in the requirements of building construction license.[123] Joint facility is a property that is not part of condominium but jointly and inseparably owned for common use.[124] Joint facility comprises meeting room, plants, landscape, social building, pray room,

118. Article 4 para. (1) of Agrarian Law.
119. Article 31 para. (4) of Land Registration Reg.
120. Article 31 para. (5) of Land Registration Reg.
121. Article 1 point 11 of Condominium Law.
122. Article 47 para. (3) of Condominium Law.
123. Article 1 point 4 of Condominium Law.
124. Article 1 point 6 of Condominium Law.

playroom, parking that is separated or integrated with the building structure. Furthermore, joint equipment is defined as parts of condominium inseparably owned for joint use in an integrated function with the condominium units.[125] Joint equipment comprises foundation, column, block, wall, floor, roof, gutter, stair, elevator, corridor, channel, pipe, electricity channel, gas, and telecommunication.

§2. Joint Ownership over Movable Property

128. ICC differentiates an ownership over goods, if the ownership is shared by more than one individual, as bound joint ownership and free joint ownership.

129. Owners of bound joint ownership are unable to do freely over the goods. According to Pitlo, in a bound jointly ownership, a good is owned by more than one individual jointly, without any purpose for them from the beginning to own the good jointly.[126] In a free joint ownership, the owners intend to jointly own a good, for example by buying the good using joint money.[127]

130. ICC stipulates that the distribution of properties, which belong to more than one person, takes place in accordance with the rules which have been described with regard to the division and distribution of inheritances.[128]

125. Article 1 point 5 of Condominium Law.

126. Kartini Muljadi and Gunawan Widjaja, *Kedudukan Berkuasa dan Hak Milik*, pp. 198–199 (1st edition. Kencana 2004).

127. *Ibid.*, p. 200.

128. Article 573 of Indonesian Civil Code.

Chapter 7. Neighbourhood and Urban Problems

131. Agrarian Law does not provide detail provisions on neighbourhood rights. This is different from ICC. ICC provides one chapter on rights and obligations among owners of neighbouring plots of land, from Articles 625–672. On those provisions, ICC stipulates that the neighbouring owners have rights and obligations arising from the location of land by its nature or by virtue of law. These provisions however are revoked since the promulgation of Agrarian Law in 1960.

132. Nevertheless, Agrarian Law stipulates essential provisions on relationship among the landowners, not only among neighbouring landowners, namely all land rights have social function.[129] Elucidation of Agrarian Law explains that the meaning of 'all land rights have social function' is that any land right held by a person is not justified that the land will be used (or will not be used) only for personal use, especially when its use damages the society. Land use must be adjusted with its circumstance and nature of its right, so that it will be useful for the prosperity and happiness of the owner as well as for the society and the state. This however does not mean that personal interest is restricted by the public interest. Social function of land means that the personal and public interest must be balanced, so that the main goals, prosperity, justice, and happiness for the people can be achieved. This provision also means that the land must be properly maintained so that its fertility will be increased and undamaged. This obligation to maintain the land is not only obligated to its owner or right holder but also to any person, legal entity, or instance that has a legal relationship with the land.[130]

133. In addition to provision of Agrarian Law, Building Law stipulates that a building constructed over, and/or below the land, water, and/or facilities and infrastructure should not disturb the environmental balance, environmental converse, and/or relevant facilities and infrastructure.[131]

134. A building must comply with comfort requirements including space for the occupants to move, air distribution in the space, view, noise and vibration levels. The comfort of view is a condition where a person's personal right in implementing activity within the building will not be disturbed by the surrounding buildings.[132] The comfort level of vibration and noise is a comfort level that will not disturb its user and the building function by the vibration and/or noise emerging within the building and its surrounding buildings.[133]

135. If the construction of building endangers the society as a result of which the society is disturbed and if it suffers losses then the society may file a class action.[134]

129. Article 6 of Agrarian Law.
130. Elucidation of Art. 6 of Agrarian Law.
131. Article 11 para. (2) of Building Law.
132. Article 26 para. (5) of Building Law.
133. Article 26 para. (6) of Building Law.
134. Article 42 para. (1) (d) of Building Law.

Chapter 8. Agrarian Problems

136. There are many agrarian problems happening in Indonesia, within the city, village, and even forest territory. The main source of Agrarian Law is customary law. Customary laws are mainly not in writing. Customary law are different among different tribes in Indonesia, even though there are sameness provision, in principle, that are then used as legal principles of agrarian. These legal principles are, among others, horizontal separation principle, nationality principle, cash, and transparent principle.

137. Determining customary law as the legal principle of agrarian causes the government to use customary law as main principle and not the western law as stipulated under ICC, and therefore, the government has to enact so many new laws and regulations so that the Agrarian Law can be implemented.

138. Despite that Agrarian Law has been promulgated more than fifty years ago, the knowledge of its main legal provisions such as types of land, obligation to register, is not unitary among the people in Indonesia. The communities living in villages and urban areas have different knowledge and perception regarding the agrarian legal provisions. These differences cause conflict of land between the parties.

139. Conflicts of land may emerge due to negative publication system used by the Agrarian Law. This system specifies that the land certificate is a strong evidence of ownership over land, but not an absolute or the only evidence of landownership. This provision alone has huge impact of loads of landownership disputes in Indonesia. An important point to note is that Indonesia does not adopt a pure negative publication system, but a negative publication system with positive element. This positive element relates to the provision stating that if within five years the party who objects the certification of land does not file his claim to the land office and to the landowner, then his right to claim can no longer be implemented.[135]

140. Many Indonesians in villages or sometimes even still in the urban areas do not have a land certificate. They may hold many names of documents, such as letter of land information, *girik*, land and building tax invoice that they regard as evidence of landownership. If a land certificate is issued over the land that they are claiming to own, a legal dispute is unavoidable.

141. Other types of agrarian problems are in the possession of huge plots of land by a certain party or group of companies but underutilized or not even utilized. This violates the legal principle of non-abandonment of land. Nevertheless, despite the existence of laws and regulations, the government or local government, and the land office, may not enforce this regulation properly. Accordingly, many unutilized lands are possessed for a long term without providing any economic benefits to the surrounding communities. This is essentially violating the justice principle of the people.

142. Dr Bernhard Limbong provides the root of land conflict in Indonesia. He divides it into general and special root-cause. The general causes are divided into legal factors and non-legal factors. The legal factors are conflicting regulations, improper regulation, conflicting courts, and disorganized bureaucracy. The non-legal factors includes conflicting usage of land, high economic value of land, escalating people's

135. Article 32 para. (2) of Land Registration Reg.

awareness, increase in the number of people without any change in the land amount, poverty. Whereas, the special causes consist of customary land issue, possession and ownership of land, land registration, land boundaries, land procurement, compensation for plantation lands, land reform, and enforcement of court decision.[136]

136. Bernhard Limbong, *Konflik Pertanahan*, p. 90 (1st edition. Margaretha Pustaka 2012).

Part II. Movable Property and Personal Property/Chattels

Chapter 1. General Classification

§1. Tangible Movable Property and Choses in Possession

143. Movable properties are tangible and non-tangible,[137] consumable or non-consumable. Consumable properties are those which disappear through use.[138]

144. Tangible properties can be viewed narrowly or widely. Narrowly, tangible properties can be touched, held, or can be seen. Widely, tangible properties include tangible property in narrow meaning and part of an asset as a result of attachment that becomes part of the property, namely:

(1) tangible property emerging from nature's production; grown from the land, such as fruits of trees; and result from or emerge from animals, such as eggs, cow's milk, whelp;
(2) man's work obtained from plantation, such as carrots, yams, peanuts.[139]

145. Possession is interpreted as the holding or enjoyment of properties, which an individual, either in person or through another person, has within the power, as if he has actual title thereto.[140] Accordingly, for a property without a definite owner, a possessor can be regarded as the owner of the property.

146. Possession may be either in good faith or in bad faith.[141] Possession will be considered that it is in good faith, if at the time the owner acquired the properties, he was unaware of the defects therein.[142] Possession is considered as possession in bad faith, if the owner is aware that the properties in his possession are not his property. This bad faith circumstance is limited from the time that a lawsuit if filed against him,

137. Article 503 of ICC.
138. Article 505 of ICC.
139. Rachmadi Usman, S.H., M.H., *Hukum Kebendaan*, p. 58 (1st edition. Sinar Grafika 2011).
140. Article 529 of ICC.
141. Article 530 of ICC.
142. Article 531 of ICC.

if the judgment is against the bad faith possessor.[143] The possessor will always be considered in good faith unless proven otherwise, with a burden to prove is on the claimant.[144]

147. To obtain a possession, one (including minors and married women) acquires it by placing properties in his power with the intention of retaining them for himself. This provision is not applicable to an insane person.[145]

148. One can acquire possessory status over a property either personally or through another person who acted on his behalf. When an individual acquires possessory status over a property through another person acted on his behalf, an individual is deemed to have acquired the possession before he is even aware that the possession of the property has been taken.[146] The possessory status of a deceased individual is, from the time of his death, passes to his heirs, together with all characteristics thereof and defects therein.[147] An individual retains possessory status, to the extent that it is not passed on to another individual, or has clearly been abandoned.[148]

149. An individual loses his possessory status voluntarily where he transfers the property to another individual.[149] An individual loses his possessory status, notwithstanding the absence of the intent to assign the properties to another person, if the individual clearly abandons such property.[150]

150. Possessory status over movable properties is lost in the following circumstances:[151]

(1) if the property is removed or stolen;
(2) if the property is lost, and the individual does not know where it is located.

151. Possessory status in good faith confers to the possessor the following rights over the property:[152]

(1) He will be deemed the owner of the property until a claim over the property is made before the judge.[153]
(2) He may obtain title to the property by lapse of time.
(3) He enjoys the gains from the properties until it is reclaimed.
(4) His possessory status must be maintained against interferences and reinstated should he lose it.

---

143. Article 532 of ICC.
144. Article 533 of ICC.
145. Articles 538 and 539 of ICC.
146. Article 540 of ICC.
147. Article 541 of ICC.
148. Article 542 of ICC.
149. Article 543 of ICC.
150. Article 544 of ICC.
151. Article 546 of ICC.
152. Article 548 of ICC.
153. Article 1977 of ICC.

152. Conversely, a possessor in bad faith also has rights over the property. They are:[154]

(1) He will be deemed the owner of the property until a claim over the property is made before the judge. This right is the same as good faith possessor.
(2) He enjoys the proceeds of the properties, provided however that he is obligated to return these to the rightful owner.
(3) His possessory status must be maintained against interferences and reinstated should he lose it.

153. The only difference in rights between good faith possessor and bad faith possessor under ICC is the ability to obtain title by lapse of time.

§2. Intangible Movable Property and Choses in Action

154. Properties are tangible and non-tangible.[155] Pursuant to law, the following are considered as movable properties:

(1) The use of the proceeds from and the use of movable properties.
(2) Fixed interests, either permanent or life interest.
(3) Agreements and claims, the object of which is claimable monetary sums or movable properties.
(4) Evidence of shares or shares in enterprises pertaining to monetary trade, commerce, or industry; notwithstanding that immovable properties, relevant to such undertakings, belong to those enterprises. Evidence of the shares or shares considered to be movable properties; however, this applies to the respective shareholders only to the extent of the duration of the association.
(5) Shares in the State's indebtedness, and those imposed on Indonesia, whether they are registered in the main ledger, or in the form of certificates, acknowledgements of debts, bonds or other stocks, with the relevant coupons or proof of interest.
(6) Shares or bonds coupons in respect of all other monetary loans, including those which were concluded by foreign entities.

155. The above-mentioned movable properties are intangible.

156. An individual loses the possessory status over intangible properties, if another person has had the peaceful enjoyment thereof for the duration of one year.[156]

§3. Funds (Capital; Investment Fund)

157. The principal law regulating fund or investment fund in Indonesia is Law Number 25 of 2007 on Capital Investment ('Capital Investment Law').

154. Article 549 of ICC.
155. Article 503 of ICC.
156. Article 547 of ICC.

158. Under Capital Investment Law, a capital is defined as an asset in the form of money or other form that is not owned by investor that has economical value.[157] The law differentiates between foreign capital and domestic capital. Foreign capital means a capital owned by a foreign state, foreigner, foreign business entity, foreign legal entity, and/or Indonesian legal entity in which its capital is partly or wholly owned by foreign parties.[158] Whereas domestic capital means a capital owned by the state of the Republic of Indonesia, Indonesian national, or business entity whether it is a legal entity or not.[159]

159. There are several legal principles of capital investment in Indonesia:

(1) Legal certainty, a principle in a legal state that uses law and regulations as its principle over every policy and action of capital investment.
(2) Transparency, it is every individual's right of society to obtain true, honest, and non-discrimination information on capital investment.
(3) Accountability, every activity and end result of capital investment must be accountable to public or society as the holder of supreme sovereignty under the prevailing laws.
(4) Same treatment, non-discrimination treatment to domestic investor and foreign investor as well as between a certain foreign investor and other foreign investor.
(5) Togetherness, a principle that enforces role of all investors to jointly realize prosperity.
(6) Fair efficiency, a basic principle for the implementation of capital investment in order to realize fair, conducive, and competitive business climate.
(7) Sustainability, a principle that in a planned manner, working the implementation of development through a capital investment to guarantee prosperity and progress in all aspects of life, today and the future.
(8) Environmental-view, a principle that investment must pay attention and prioritize the protection and care over environment.
(9) Independency, a principle to enhance the state's and nations' potential by not closing itself from foreign investment, for the interest of economic development.
(10) Progress and unity of national economy balance, a principle to maintain balance of economic progress within the state.[160]

160. Investment conducted by domestic and foreign investors through a limited liability company, can be by:

(1) subscribing shares by the time a limited liability company is established;
(2) buying shares; and
(3) doing other means according to laws and regulations.[161]

---

157. Article 1 Number 7 of Capital Investment Law.
158. Article 1 Number 8 of Capital Investment Law.
159. Article 1 Number 9 of Capital Investment Law.
160. Elucidation of Article of Capital Investment Law.
161. Article 5 para. (3) of Capital Investment Law.

161. Every investor is entitled to do a transfer and repatriation in foreign exchange, for:

(1) Capital.
(2) Profit, bank's interest, dividend, and other income.
(3) Fund required for: (i) raw and auxiliary materials, half-made goods, or made goods; or (ii) replacement of capital goods to maintain investment.
(4) Capital addition for investment.
(5) Fund to repay loan.
(6) Royalty or other payable expense.
(7) Revenue from foreigner working in the capital investment company.
(8) Sales proceed or liquidation of investment.
(9) Compensation over losses.
(10) Compensation over take over.
(11) Payment made for technical assistance, payable expenses for technical and management service, payment for project, and intellectual property right.
(12) Sales proceed of asset sale.[162]

§4. Chattels Personal and Chattels Real

162. If the law or any other civil deed uses the terms 'movable properties', 'household furnishings', 'furniture' or 'household goods', 'furnishing', or 'a house fully furnished', without any addition, expansion or limitation, the aforementioned terms deemed to include the objects as set out below.[163]

163. 'Movable properties' include, without exception, any objects that, according to the regulations, are regarded as movable.[164]

164. 'Household furnishings' include anything that is regarded as movable under 'movable properties' with the exception of ready cash, shares, debts, and other rights as mentioned in Article 511 of ICC, regarding trade and basis material, implements for factories, factory's production, or agricultural products, building material designated for construction or resulting from demolition, as well as ships and ship's shares.[165]

165. 'Furniture' or 'household goods' includes everything, which is included as 'household furnishings', with the exception of horses and livestock, carriages and their equipment, precious stones, books and writings, drawings, prints, paintings, statutes, commemorative medal scientific equipment, and other valuables and curiosities, personal clothing, weapons, grains, wine and other means of livelihood.[166]

166. The expression of 'a house with all its furnishings' includes everything, which qualifies as 'movable properties' and is located in the house, with the exception of ready cash and document in respect of indebtedness and other rights which might

162. Article 8 para. (3) of Capital Investment Law.
163. Article 512 of ICC.
164. Article 513 of ICC.
165. Article 514 of ICC.
166. Article 515 of ICC.

be found in the house.[167] Further, the expressions 'furnishing' includes furniture, which is used and which decorates the rooms, such as wallpaper and carpets, beds, chairs, mirrors, clocks, tables, porcelain, and other objects of that nature. Paintings and statues, which form part of the furniture of a room, are also included in the term 'furnishing', but the collection of paintings, prints, and statutes which are displayed in galleries and special rooms is excluded. This is also applicable to porcelain; those which comprise part of the decorations of a room are included in the term 'furnishing'.[168] The term 'a furnished house' or 'a house with furniture' only covers the furnishings.[169]

167. Right similar to chattels real is governed under ICC and Agrarian Law. There are leases for movable and immovable properties.

168. Agrarian Law stipulates lease over the land. Right of lease for building means a right of lease over land, where the lessee is authorized to use other party's land for building purpose, by paying to the landlord a definite amount of rent. The rental payment can be made one time or on a certain time, or before or after the land is used. This land lease agreement cannot be accompanied with conditions that contain extortion elements.[170]

169. Limitation on lease, not containing extortion elements, emerges from a principle, where each person has to utilize his own farm. That provision is intended to protect the weak. Land usage on the ground of lease, profit sharing, pledge, and other means cannot be freely agreed by the parties, but the government must stipulate its terms and conditions to achieve justice and prevent exploitation.[171]

170. Agrarian Law explains that right of lease is a right of use that has special characters. Right of lease is only provided for buildings. Lease over farm is only temporary. The state cannot lease land since the state is not the owner of land.[172]

171. Holders of right of lease for building are Indonesian nationals, foreigners domiciled in Indonesia, legal entities established and domiciled in Indonesia, and foreign legal entity having its representative in Indonesia.[173]

172. A house and a condominium unit can be leased. Law Number 1 of 2011 on Housing and Residential Areas ('Housing Law') stipulates that right to occupy a house can be through ownership or with lease or without lease.[174] A foreigner can occupy a house through right of lease or right of use.[175]

173. Similar provision is applicable to a condominium unit regulated under Condominium Law. Control over commercial-type condominium unit[176] can be through ownership or lease. Lease over condominium unit consists of personal right over condominium unit and utilization over joint facility, joint equipment, and joint land.

---

167. Article 516 of ICC.
168. Article 517 of ICC.
169. Article 518 of ICC.
170. Article 44 of Agrarian Law.
171. Chapter II Number 7 of General Elucidation of Agrarian Law.
172. Elucidation of Art. 44 of Agrarian Law.
173. Article 45 of Agrarian Law.
174. Article 50 para. (2) of Housing Law.
175. Article 52 para. (1) of Housing Law.
176. Commercial condominium means a condominium that is constructed for profit (Art. 1 point 10 of Condominium Law).

A lease agreement over condominium unit within public condominium and commercial condominium must be made before a Notary and registered to Association of Owner and Tenant of Condominium Unit ('P3SRS').[177]

177. Article 45 paras (1), (4) and (5) of Condominium Law.

Chapter 2. Legal Interests

174. There are ten principles of Indonesian property law, namely:

(1) Property law is compulsory and cannot be waived by the parties.
(2) Right to property can be transferred, meaning that, as long as it does not violate laws, public order, and morality, property right can be transferred from the previous owner to the other party, with all its consequences.
(3) Individual, meaning that what can be owned as property is all things that according to law can be separated.
(4) Totality, meaning that individual ownership over property also means comprehensive ownership of each part of the property. In this context, for example, a person may be unable to have part-ownership over a property if one does not own a comprehensive ownership over a property.
(5) Inseparable. This principle is as a consequence of totality principle, which it is not possible for an individual to relinquish partly of his right over a property. Even though an owner is authorized to pledge its ownership with other property right that is limited (*jura in re aliena*), that pledge can only be made for the whole property. *Jura in re aliena* cannot be made only for property's part.
(6) Priority, meaning that there is level of priority over limited property rights.
(7) Mixture, meaning that an owner of property which is pledged with limited property right (*jura in re aliena*) cannot be the owner or holder of the limited property right. If the limited property right is assigned to the owner of the property, then the limited property right will be voided.
(8) Publicity, that is applicable to immovable right granted a property right.
(9) Different treatment principle over movable and immovable property right.
(10) Existence of nature of agreement in every procurement or formation of property right. This principle reminds us that every law of agreement also contains property right and each property right is also attached by its agreement law within. The nature of agreement is becoming more important due to granting of limited property right (*jura in re aliena*) as set out by the laws and regulations.[178]

175. Property law is also called as civil right. Civil right consists of absolute right (*ius in re*) and relative right (*ius ad rem*). Absolute right is a right that is applicable and must be honoured by every individual that is part of civil right. Absolute right is divided into several elements:

(1) Absolute right over property, called as property right regulated under Book II of ICC.
(2) Absolute right that is also related to individual's personal right, called as personal right, such as right to life, right to be free, etc.

178. Kartini Mulyadi & Gunawan Widjaya, *Kebendaan pada Umumnya*, p. 228 (1st edition. Kencana 2003).

(3) Absolute right related to individual and family, called as family right, such as right occurred as a result of relationship between parents and children, guardian and child, etc.
(4) Absolute right of intangible property, called as *immaterieel recht*, such as trademark, patents, copyright.[179]

176. In addition to absolute right, relative right is also part of civil right, that is within personal right and strongly related to obligation law as stipulated in Book III of ICC. Personal right means all rights occurred as a result of loan relationship, and in contrast, loan may derive from agreement, laws, and other sources.[180]

177. Property right is absolute, in which where there is hindrance by third party, the owner of a property can execute his rights against any parties. The owner of a property can implement his rights against anyone who disturbs him, and the disturber can be warned by the owner based on his property right. This means that in each property right there is a direct relationship between an individual and his property, even though there is interference by other party. In contrast, for personal right that is relative, it can only be implemented against a definite party that is bound to an agreement. This means that within each personal right, there is relationship among individuals, even though a property is seen through a legal relationship.[181]

178. According to Subekti, a property right is a right that provides direct authority over a property, such authority can be upheld against every person.[182] The same provision is explained by Sri Soedewi Masjchoen Sofwan, a property right is absolute right over property of which such right grants direct authority over a property and can be maintained against anyone.[183]

179. Property right gives powers over a property, meaning that property right is related to its property, even though there is interference by outsider. Where personal right gives a claim over performance by the other party that can be upheld against definite individual or party.[184]

---

179. Rachmadi Usman, S.H., M.H., *Hukum Jaminan Keperdataan*, pp. 105–106 (1st edition. Sinar Grafika 2008).
180. *Ibid.*, p. 106.
181. *Ibid.*, p. 107 (1st edition. Sinar Grafika 2008).
182. Subekti, *Pokok-Pokok Hukum Perdata*, p. 52 (Intermasa 1979).
183. Rachmadi Usman, S.H., M.H., *Hukum Jaminan Keperdataan*, p. 109 (1st edition. Sinar Grafika 2008).
184. *Ibid.*, p. 109.

Chapter 3. Equitable Interests

180. The legal concept of equitable interests is similar to possession of movable property and to acquire legal right out of the movable property. This issue has been described in Part II, Chapter 1, §1 Tangible Movable Property and Choses in Possession, and §2 Intangible Movable Property and Choses in Action, as well as in Part III, Chapter 3.

Chapter 4. Security Interests

181. 'Security' is a translation of '*zekerheid*' or '*causie*' which means a debtor's capacity to fulfil or complete his debts to the creditor, by way of withholding certain property with economical value as security over loan or credit which has been received by the debtor from the creditor.[185]

182. Mariam Darus Badrulzaman says that security is a surety by the debtor and/or third party to the creditor to secure his obligations in an agreement.[186] A similar statement is provided by Hartono Hadisoeprapto, who says that security means something given by the debtor to the creditor to convince that the debtor will fulfil his obligation that can be valued with money emerging from an agreement.[187]

183. Security over a movable property can be made through a fiduciary security and pledge. A pledge is a right which is obtained by a creditor in a movable asset, which has been provided to him by the debtor or his proxy, to secure his debt, and which authorizes the creditor's priority over the other creditors with regard to the settlement of the debt; with the exception of the costs incurred in the sale of the asset and the costs for the maintenance of the pledged asset and of which must be prioritized.[188] Whereas fiduciary security means security right over movable property, tangible or intangible and immovable property especially building, that cannot be pledged with mortgage right which is possessed by the debtor, as security over certain debt, that give preferential position to the creditor against the other creditors.[189]

184. Shares in the limited liability company are categorized as intangible movable property and regarded as property right which can be upheld against any party. Under Law Number 40 of 2007 on Limited Liability Company ('Company Law'), shares can be encumbered through a pledge or fiduciary security to the extent there are no other provisions in its articles of association stipulate otherwise. The pledge or fiduciary security over shares that has been registered in accordance with the prevailing laws and regulations must be recorded in the shareholder register and special register.[190] The recordation is important so that third party who has interest in the shares can understand legal status of the shares. Information recorded contains information on the grantee of fiducia of shares and date of registration over fiduciary security.[191] Voting right over pledged shares or encumbered with fiduciary security vests with the shareholder.[192]

185. *Ibid.*, p. 66.
186. Mariam Darus Badrulzaman, *Beberapa Permasalahan Hukum Hak Jaminan*, p. 12 (Yayasan Pengembangan Hukum Bisnis 2000).
187. Hartono Hadisoeprapto, *Seri Hukum Perdata: Pokok-Pokok Hukum Perdata dan Hukum Jaminan*, p. 50 (Indhill-Co. 1984).
188. Article 1150 of ICC.
189. Article 1 point 2 of Fiducia Law.
190. Article 60 of Company Law.
191. Article 50 para. (1) (d) of Company Law.
192. Article 60 para. (4) of Company Law.

Part III. Acquisition of Property Rights

Chapter 1. Transfer of Property by Contract Inter Vivos

185. ICC stipulates that no individual can represent a living person.[193]

193. Article 847 of ICC.

Chapter 2. Transfer of Property by Death

186. Inheritance only occurs by death.[194] The heirs is by law assume possession of the properties, rights, and lawsuits of the deceased. If there is a dispute over who shall be the heirs, and who shall be authorized to hold title to the property, the judge may order that the properties shall be held in the court's safekeeping. The state must try to place itself as a possessor by the judge, and is obligated to instruct seizure of inheritance assets, and to prepare their details, in the form determined for receipt of inheritance with special right of assets' detail, failure to do so is penalized with costs, losses, and interests.[195]

187. For land rights, the transfer of right due to inheritance needs to be registered. This provision is regulated under Land Registration Reg. This transfer may happen for registered land rights, unregistered land rights, or right of ownership over condominium unit. To register the transfer, the heirs have to submit the relevant land right, a death certificate of the inheritor, and evidence as an heir. The transfer of right due to inheritance occurs by virtue of law at the time the right holder passed away. This means that the heirs will become the new owner of land right. The stipulation of who becomes the official heir is regulated under the civil law applicable to the inheritor. This registration of transfer is compulsory to protect the heirs and for order of land registration, so that the data shown is up-to-date. The evidence of an heir can be in the form of deed of information over inheritance right, or determination letter of heirs or letter of information of heirs.[196]

188. Regulation of State Minister of Agrarian/Chairman of National Land Office Number 3 of 1997 on Implementing Provisions of Government Regulation Number 24 of 1997 on Land Registration ('MR 3/1997') stipulates that for transfer of immovable property due to inheritance, the evidence as heir for Indonesian genuine citizen is a letter of inheritance made by all heirs witnessed by two witnesses and strengthened by the chief of village/sub-district office and Camat located at the domicile of the inheritor; for Indonesian of Chinese descendant, a deed of inheritance from the Notary; for Indonesian citizen of foreign east descendant, a letter of inheritance from the Treasure Hall (*Balai Harta Peninggalan*).[197]

194. Article 830 of ICC.
195. Article 833 of ICC.
196. Article 42 and its elucidation of Land Registration Reg.
197. Article 11 para. (1) (c) of MR 3/1997.

Chapter 3. Possession

189. Possession is a means to obtain ownership right over property that is not possessed and/or ownership of other person.[198]

190. There exists properties which do not belong to anybody; all other properties are the property of the State, or of communities, or of specific individuals.[199] This provision is applicable to movable properties only since 1960, because Agrarian Law regulates that the State does not have ownership over land, but only controlling right.

191. Properties belonging to a community are those which are the common property of an association.[200] Properties belonging to specific individuals are those which comprise the separate property of one or more individuals.[201]

192. Movable properties, which are not within any individual's ownership, shall become the property of the individual who shall be the first to appropriate them.[202] This provision relates to Article 1977 paragraph (1) of ICC which states that with regard to movable properties which do not comprise interests or debts which are not payable to bearer, the possession of such is deemed as absolute ownership.

193. It is noted that the possession process to become ownership over movable property is reduced so that all forms of possession, unless proven otherwise, is deemed as ownership over that property.[203]

194. For land, Agrarian Law does not recognize possession through an expiry as a means to obtain ownership over land. This is fundamentally different than what has been stipulated under ICC which regulates that ownership may be acquired by expiry, if he has possessed it as stipulated by laws and according to requirement as set out in ICC.[204] ICC further stipulates that, to acquire ownership of property by means of expiry, an individual must have continuous, uninterrupted, open, and unequivocal possession,[205] unless the possession was derived from acts of violence, arbitrary, or ignorant.[206] An individual, who in good faith, acquires immovable property, interests, or several other acknowledgements of indebtedness which do not have to be paid to bearer, acquires ownership thereof through expiry, after possessing it for a period of twenty years.[207] ICC further stipulates that an individual, who in good faith possesses something for thirty years, acquires ownership thereof, without having to prove its title.[208]

---

198. Kartini Muljadi and Gunawan Widjaja, *Kedudukan Berkuasa dan Hak Milik*, p. 152 (1st edition. Kencana 2004).
199. Article 519 of ICC.
200. Article 526 of ICC.
201. Article 527 of ICC.
202. Article 585 of ICC.
203. Kartini Muljadi and Gunawan Widjaja, *Kedudukan Berkuasa dan Hak Milik*, p. 155 (1st edition. Kencana 2004).
204. Article 610 of ICC.
205. Article 1955 of ICC.
206. Article 1956 of ICC.
207. Article 1963 para. (1) of ICC.
208. Article 1963 para. (2) of ICC.

195. The above provision to acquire ownership of land after possession of twenty consecutive years, despite not recognized under Agrarian Law, is regulated under Land Registration Reg. Land Registration Reg. stipulates that if there is no complete evidence to apply ownership of land, the right registration can be made based on the actual physical control over land for twenty consecutive years or more by the applicant and its predecessors, provided that the control is conducted in good faith and transparent by the applicant as the rightful owner of land, and strengthened by the trustworthy witness, and that control of land is not disputed by customary communities or village/sub-district or any other party before and during the announcement of land certification. This provision is considered as a leeway if the applicant is unable to provide any evidences for the ownership of land, in writing or other form of reliable evidence.[209]

196. Agrarian Law sourcing from customary law does not recognize ownership of right through an expiry means or also called as '*acquisitieve verjaring*'. Under customary law, what is recognized is a *rechtsverwerking* institution,[210] which means otherwise, namely by the expiry of time causing that person loses his right over land that previously owned by him.[211]

197. The *rechtsverwerking* concept is upheld by the decision of Hoog Gerechts Hof (HGH) dated 25 October 1934. Below are several other court decisions on *rechtsverwerking*:

(1) The claim is unacceptable, since the claimant by abandoning his land for twenty-five years, must be deemed as relinquishing his rights (*rechtsverwerking*). The Supreme Court considers that the buyer of farm should be protected, since it may be deemed, that he is acting in good faith in purchasing the farm from the heirs of deceased owner of farm (Decision Number 210/K/Sip/1955).

(2) Supreme Court can agree opinion of *judex facti*, namely, even though the claimant is still under age, his mother, as trustee, is obligated to maintain the right of the claimant until he becomes adult, and in this case, his mother was negligent so that the land was possessed by the defendant for around eighteen years, and due to her negligence, she is considered relinquishing his right (*rechtsverwerking*) over land (Decision Number 239/K/Sip/1957).[212]

---

209. Article 24 para. (2) and its elucidation of Land Registration Reg.

210. Supreme Court decision Number 329 K/SIP/1957 dated 24 Sept. 1958 with a legal principle, in South Tapanuli, if a plot of land, acquired from the forest, for five year consecutively is abandoned by the rightful owner, then that land right is deemed to be relinquished and that land by the chief of community may be granted to other person.

211. Prof. Boedi Harsono, *Hukum Agraria Indonesia: Sejarah Pembentukan Undang-Undang Pokok Agraria, Isi dan Pelaksanaannya*, p. 325 (revised edition. Djambatan 2008).

212. *Ibid.*, p. 67.

Chapter 4. Accession

198. Anything that, due to a property right, comprises part of a property, including products, either produced naturally or through labour, to the extent that these are attached to the branch or roots, or attached to the soil, deemed to comprise part of the property.[213] For immovable property, this accession principle is no longer applicable. Agrarian Law does not recognize accession as means to acquire property since its customary law recognizes horizontal separation principle, meaning that the building is not by itself owned by the owner of land, even though it is built right over the land.

199. Proceeds as a result of civil relationship are considered to be part of the property, to the extent that they are not claimable, without prejudice to special legal regulations and agreements.[214]

200. Anything attached to or which forms part of property, shall belong to its owner.[215] This provision is also related to the obligation to deliver a property, which stipulates that it also includes all things that are its equipment and intended for its permanent use, together with ownership letter, if any.[216]

201. For land, this legal principle is not applicable. Since Agrarian Law was promulgated in 1960, the building or plants constructed or planted over the land are not automatically regarded as ownership of the landowner. This is based on a horizontal separation principle of customary law of Indonesia. Despite this principle, it is possible in practice that a legal action over land also includes building and plants over its, provided that the building and plants are physically integrated with the land, meaning that the building is having foundation and the plant is considered as hard plants; building and plants are owned by the landlord; and the intent is clearly mentioned in the deed proving that legal action.[217]

213. Article 500 of ICC.
214. Article 501 of ICC.
215. Article 588 of ICC.
216. Article 1482 of ICC.
217. Prof. Boedi Harsono, *Hukum Agraria Indonesia: Sejarah Pembentukan Undang-Undang Pokok Agraria, Isi dan Pelaksanaannya*, p. 263 (revised edition. Djambatan 2008).

Chapter 5. Appropriation

202. Appropriation is not specifically regulated under ICC, but in several other laws. Company Law stipulates that a limited liability company means a legal entity as a capital alliance, set up according to an agreement, doing business activity with an authorized capital divided by shares.[218] It further stipulates that a shareholder of a limited liability company is not responsible personally for the agreements made on behalf of the company and is not responsible for the company's losses more than the owned shares.[219] This provision clearly regulates that there is a separation of shares paid to the company, and then becomes capital of the company, with the personal assets of the shareholders. The two items are not mixed and integrated, but separated. This understanding is further explained under elucidation of Article 3 of Company Law saying that a shareholder is only responsible limited to his owned shares and does not include his personal assets. This provision is applicable to any legal subject, an individual or legal entity.[220]

203. There is an exception over limited liability of shareholder, if:

(1) requirements as legal entity has not been fulfilled yet;
(2) the respective shareholder directly or indirectly, with a bad faith, use the company for his personal interest;
(3) the respective shareholder is involved in the unlawful act made by the company; or
(4) the respective shareholder directly or indirectly, unlawfully, use company's assets, and causes company's assets become inadequate to repay its loan.

The limited liability principle may be waived if proved that the company is set up only as a tool used by the shareholder to fulfil his personal interest.[221]

204. Similar provisions can be seen in the foundation and state-owned enterprises legal concept. A foundation is regulated under Law Number 16 of 2001 on Foundation as lastly amended by Law Number 28 of 2004 ('Foundation Law'). A foundation means a legal entity consisting of a separated asset and intended to fulfil certain purpose socially, religiously, and humanity, which does not have any member.[222] The Foundation Law further stipulates that a foundation is founded by one or more individuals by separating part of founder's asset, as initial asset.[223] The key word is separation of asset, from the founder to the foundation which will become a legal entity.

205. State-owned enterprises are regulated under Law Number 19 of 2003 on State-owned Enterprises ('SOE Law'). State-owned enterprise is defined as a business entity, whose capital is wholly or partly owned by the state through direct investment

218. Article 1 Number 1 of Company Law.
219. Article 3 para. (1) of Company Law.
220. Elucidation of Art. 3 para. (1) of Company Law.
221. Article 3 para. (3) and its elucidation of Company Law.
222. Article 1 Number 1 of Foundation Law.
223. Article 9 para. (1) of Foundation Law.

deriving from a separated state's asset.[224] This separated asset is state's asset from the state budget.

224. Article 1 Number 1 of SOE Law.

Chapter 6. Expropriation

206. Expropriation is mainly regulated for immovable property with regard to civil relationship, namely revocation of land right as stipulated under Law Number 20 of 1961 on Revocation of Rights of Land

207. and Properties over It ('Land Revocation Law') and land procurement as stipulated under Law Number 2 of 2012 on Land Procurement for Public Interest ('Land Procurement Law').

208. Other types of expropriation for movable property with regard to civil relationship are not regulated. Under Land Revocation Law and Land Procurement Law, the compensation is only given for the immovable properties and other properties related to the land, such as plants and buildings.

209. Nevertheless, ICC clearly regulates that ownership right can be expropriated for public interest.[225] This provision has to be interpreted to include movable and immovable properties, prior to 1960 on the promulgation date of Agrarian Law. After that date, this provision is only applicable for movable properties since for land right, the legal basis would be Agrarian Law, Land Revocation Law promulgated in 1961, and then eventually Land Procurement Law in 2012.

210. For movable properties, they can be expropriated by the state, without compensation, as a result of extraordinary criminal offence such as money laundering and corruption. Money laundering is regulated under Law Number 8 of 2010 on Prevention and Eradication of Money Laundering Criminal Offense ('Money Laundering Law'), whereas corruption is regulated under Law Number 31 of 1999 on Eradication of Corruption Criminal Offense as amended by Law Number 20 of 2011 ('Corruption Law').

211. Land Revocation Law stipulates that for public interest, including the interest of the nation and state as well as joint public interest of the people, as well as development interest, the President in urgent circumstance, after listening to Minister of Agrarian, Minister of Justice and relevant Ministers, is able to revoke land rights and properties over it.[226] The possession over land and/or related properties over the land can only be conducted after the letter of revocation of right from the President is issued and after payment of compensation, as set forth in the aforementioned letter, as well as the shelter plan for the people whose rights are being revoked, cultivators, or tenants.[227]

212. Expropriation of land can happen not only due to revocation of right or voluntary relinquishment but also as a result of abandonment. All types of land rights, such as right of ownership, right to build, right to cultivate, right of use may be revoked due to either revocation of land right or land abandonment. Revocation is stipulated under Land Revocation Law. Abandonment of land which results to cancellation of land right is regulated under government regulation.

213. Land Procurement Law, despite having similar intent with the Land Revocation Law, has different mechanism of how the land is procured from the landowners. If the Land Revocation Law clearly stipulates that the land right can be revoked, the Land Procurement Law procures the land right to a land right relinquishment from the landowners to the state, and then the procurer of land will apply to the state for land certification.

214. Land procurement for public interest is conducted for the development of:

---

225. Article 570 of ICC.
226. Article 1 of Land Revocation Law.
227. Article 5 of Land Revocation Law.

(1) National defence and security.
(2) Public road, toll road, tunnel, railroad, rail station, and train operational facility.
(3) Reservoir, dam, irrigation, drinkable water channel, waste water channel and sanitation, and other irrigation building.
(4) Seaport, airport, and terminal.
(5) Oil, gas, and geothermal infrastructure.
(6) Electricity power plant, transmission, relay station, network, and its distribution.
(7) Telecommunication and information network of the government.
(8) Landfill.
(9) Central or regional government-owned hospital.
(10) Public safety facility.
(11) Central or regional government-owned memorial land.
(12) Social facility, public facility, and greenery space.
(13) Natural reserve and cultural heritage.
(14) Central or regional government, or village office.
(15) Consolidation of slums area, land consolidation, and housing for low-income communities.
(16) Central or regional government-owned educational facility or school.
(17) Central or regional government-owned sport facility.
(18) Public market and public parking space.[228]

215. All developments, except for national defence and security, as a result of land procurement as mentioned above must be conducted by the government, and the government can cooperate with state-owned enterprises, regional government-owned enterprises or private companies.

228. Article 10 of Land Procurement Law.

Chapter 7. Insolvency

216. There is no specific meaning of insolvency or insolvent under Indonesian law even though the term has been used in various laws and regulations. Bankruptcy Law does not give a boundary of its meaning, but provide elucidation that insolvency means a condition of inability to pay.[229] Collins dictionary provides similar understanding, as having insufficient assets to meet debts and liabilities.[230]

217. Under Bankruptcy Law, a bankrupt's assets will be considered as insolvent if there is no restructuring proposal in a meeting to match receivables, the restructuring proposal is declined, or legalization of settlement is declined based on the final and binding court's decision.[231] In a postponement of debt payment obligation, which is also regulated under Bankruptcy Law, if there is a settlement within that process, but the settlement is not implemented, or the legalization over settlement is declined by the court by reasons – that debtor's assets are a lot larger that the agreed amount in the settlement; the implementation of settlement is not satisfactory; settlement was reached due to a fraud, or collusion with one or more creditors, or other dishonest means and without regard to whether the debtor or other party cooperates to reach it; and/or reward of fees and expenses spent by the expert and administrator have not been paid or no guarantee was given for it – and the debtor is decided as bankrupt, then the same insolvent condition will be immediately operative.[232]

218. If a creditor relieves one of the debtors in a joint and several obligations, and one of them becomes insolvent, the share of the insolvent debtor will be borne by the other debtors on a pro-rata basis, including those debtors who were relieved from the joint and several obligations.[233]

219. In a novation, ICC stipulates that a creditor, who has released a debtor who transferred his obligation, is not entitled to claim against that person if the substitute becomes bankrupt or insolvent, unless such right to claim has been expressly retained in the agreement, or if the substitute debtor at the time of transfer is clearly bankrupt, or if his estate is in a state of continuous decline.[234] The same provision also applies for a transfer of receivables. ICC stipulates that if the seller of receivables has promised to guarantee the capability of debtor to pay his debt, then seller's promise must be construed as promise over debtor's ability at the time of sale, and not of future circumstance unless agreed otherwise specifically.[235]

220. In a guarantee agreement, ICC stipulates that a debtor, who is required to provide a guarantor, must present a capable person to bind himself to an agreement, or to fulfil his agreement and domiciled in Indonesia.[236] ICC stipulates further that if

---

229. Elucidation of Art. 57 para. (1) of Bankruptcy Law.
230. At https://www.collinsdictionary.com/dictionary/english/insolvent, accessed on 30 Oct. 2017.
231. Article 178 para. (1) of Bankruptcy Law.
232. Article 292 of Bankruptcy Law.
233. Article 1294 of ICC.
234. Article 1418 of ICC.
235. Article 1536 of ICC.
236. Article 1827 of ICC.

the guarantor who is accepted by the creditor voluntarily or based on the judge's decision thereafter becomes insolvent, then a new guarantor must be appointed.[237]

221. All properties must be sold in public in accordance with the prevailing laws and regulations.[238] If this public sale is not achieved then a private sale can be made with a permission of supervisory judge.[239] Through this public sale or private sale, the bankrupt asset can then be transferred to third party.

237. Article 1829 of ICC.
238. Article 185 para. (1) of Bankruptcy Law.
239. Article 185 para. (2) of Bankruptcy Law.

Part IV. Trust and Fiduciary Mechanisms

Chapter 1. Administration of Property. Fiducia Cum Amico

222. Fiduciary Security Law does not specifically stipulate or recognize the legal concept of *fiducia cum amico*. But one can see similar provisions regulated under ICC.

223. ICC divides that a legal relation may derive from a law or an agreement. If the legal relation derives from the law, ICC divides it as legal relation deriving from only law or laws as a result of individual's action. This legal relation may be emerged as a result of valid action or unlawful action.[240]

224. Lawmakers explain several legal relations emerged from the law as a result of individual's legitimate action, such as representing other individual's interest (*zaakwaarneming*), payment of non-compulsory debt (*onverschuldigde betaling*) causing enrichment without a valid right, and free or appropriate legal relation (*natuurlijke verbintenis*). These legal relations do not subject to the validity elements of an agreement since these legal relations are derived from the law.[241]

225. ICC stipulates that if an individual, voluntarily, without having been assigned thereto, manages the affairs of a person with or without the knowledge of that person, he is impliedly binds himself to continue and complete the management, until the person whose interests are managed is in a position to manage such affairs himself.[242]

226. Characteristics of managing other person's interest voluntarily are as follows:

(1) This figure is one of the legal relations deriving from the law, occurring as a result of an individual's legitimate action. This figure is not subject to Article 1320 of ICC.
(2) The party managing other person's interest is called as *gestor*. The party whose interests or affairs are managed is called as *dominus*.
(3) This figure is different from the granting of proxy since proxy is based on an agreement.

240. Article 1353 of ICC.
241. Prof. Dr Mariam Darus Badrulzaman, *Hukum Perikatan dalam KUH Perdata Buku Ketiga*, p. 136 (1st edition. Citra Aditya Bakti 2015).
242. Article 1354 of ICC.

(4) The difference between granting of proxy is that it is an agreement where a person giving proxy to other person, accepting it for an on behalf of the grantor to do something.

The difference between voluntary management and granting of proxy is that to represent other person, that person must voluntarily do it without any instruction. Voluntary means his own willingness to assist, a service without regard of money, but appropriateness. Therefore, as a consequence, that person does not obtain any payment[243] whereas in granting a proxy, the authorized may obtain fees.[244]

227. ICC further stipulates that this gestor is obligated to continue his management, notwithstanding that the person whose interest he has assumed may pass away prior to the completion of the matter, until such time that the heir can take over such management. This provision is similar to provisions to an authorized.[245] On that matter, ICC stipulates that the authorized (a person receiving a proxy), as long as the proxy has not been revoked yet, is obligated to implement his proxy and is responsible to all expenses, losses, and interest occurring as a result of its non-implementation. He must also finalize any matter which he has commenced at the time the authorizer passes away, if loss could occur as a result of not finalizing the matter immediately.[246] Both gestor and authorized are obligated to continue and finish his management even though the person whose interest is represented has passed away. The only exception is, since proxy is not a voluntary management, this particular obligation ceases if the proxy is revoked by the heirs.

228. The gestor is obligated, with respect to such management, to fulfil the obligations in the manner of a proper head of a household.[247] Nevertheless, the judge is authorized to reduce the compensation of costs, damages, and interest resulting from the error or negligence of the gestor, depending upon the circumstances, which have caused him to manage the affairs.[248]

229. The person whose interest have been properly managed or *dominus*, is bound to fulfil any obligation, which has been concluded by the *gestor* on his behalf, and provides indemnification and interest caused by all legal relations that individual made by him, and reimburse all necessary expenses.[249]

243. Article 1358 of ICC.
244. *Ibid.*, p. 137.
245. Article 1355 of ICC.
246. Article 1800 of ICC.
247. Article 1356 para. (1) of ICC.
248. Article 1356 para. (2) of ICC.
249. Article 1357 of ICC.

Chapter 2. Security. Fiducia Cum Creditore (see also Parts I, II and V)

230. During Roman period, a granting of security to secure implementation of an agreement can only be made by way of transferring ownership over secured property to the creditor, named as *fiducia cum creditore*. From the word 'cum creditore' the aforementioned delivery is not intended for the transfer of right, but only as security, not to be owned by the creditor, and according to that security institution, a creditor does not have the authority as owner. After the debtor fulfils his obligations set forth under the agreement, the creditor is obligated to return the secured property to the debtor. Since debtor acted on a basis of trust that the creditor, after receipt of repayment of loan will not violate his promise by owning the secured property, (and consider himself as the absolute owner) the relationship is then called as fides relationship or fiducia relationship.[250]

231. After another security institution is developed, such as pledge and hypothec, and then the means of security of *fiducia cum creditore* is not popular anymore. At the end of nineteenth century, an event emerged that causes a necessity for the security institution other than pledge, even though the pledged property is a movable property. At that period, there was a crisis for agriculture business as a result of pest attack so that the agricultural entrepreneurs require capital assistance from a bank. At that time, the bank can only provide loan with a security in the form of pledge of farming tools. This is hard to fulfil since the farmers require those tools to do their production. They were also unable to provide hypothec since they do not have land. In addition, bank also requires additional security other than hypothec. That condition yielded a new security institution called as *Oogsteverband* (harvest bound), where the harvest yield is secured as additional security. Since the harvest yield is movable property, then prior to *Oogstverband*, the security institution to be used should have been a pledge, with a consequence that the pledged property must be removed from the possession of the pledger. Currently, *Oogstverband* also provides possibility for the security of movable property that is kept by the security grantor. This is the first step of the emergence of fiducia institution.[251]

232. Many authors call fiduciary security by various names, depending on which to emphasize, among others:

(1) *Fiducia cum creditore* (Roman period).
(2) *Bezitloos pand* (pledge without possession), since the possessor is the debtor but not as owner.
(3) *Een verkapt pandrecht* (concealed pledge).
(4) *Uitbouw* (expansion of pledge).
(5) *Zekerheidseigendom* (ownership right only as a pledge) or *fiduciaire eigendom* (ownership based on trust) or *uitgeholde eigendom* (reduce ownership right).

250. J. Satrio, S.H., *Hukum Jaminan Hak Jaminan Kebendaan*, pp. 166–167 (Citra Aditya Bakti 1996).
251. *Ibid.*, pp. 167–168 (Citra Aditya Bakti 1996).

(6) *Bezitloos zekerheidsrecht* (security right without possession).
(7) *Verruimd pandbegrip* (expanded meaning of pledge).
(8) *Eigendomsoverdracht tot zekerheid* (delivery of ownership right as security).
(9) *Voorraadpand.*
(10) *Pandrechtverruiming* (expanded pledge).
(11) *Hypotheek of roerend goed* (*bezitloos pandrecht*).[252]

233. Fiducia institution in Indonesia for the first time deemed as permissible through a decision of HgH. Dated 18 August 1932[253] on a legal case between *B.P.M* against *Clignet*, where it is said that under title XX of Book II ICC there are stipulations of pledge, but they do not prevent the parties to form other agreement other than pledge agreement, if the pledge agreement is not suitable to regulate the legal relationship between the parties. Fiducia agreement is considered granting security and is not regarded as pledge agreement. HgH thus considers, since fiducia is not a pledge agreement, that it does not have to adhere to pledge elements.[254]

234. There are several characters of fiducia. Fiducia as institution is in practice implemented by means of, the debtor grants the security to the creditor for debtor's promises (especially promise on time and mechanism of repayment of loan), delivers his ownership over security based on trust to the creditor, but with a promise, if the debtor has fulfilled all his obligations, particularly to repay the loan as promised, then the ownership right of property will automatically be transferred to the debtor. This fiduciary security takes the form of 'delivery of ownership right based on trust' or can be called as *fiduciaire eigendoms-overdracht*.[255]

235. Question arises, if the delivery is made, will the creditor become the owner of secured property? It must be remembered that the intent of this type of security is to provide security. Hence, the creditor does not become actual owner at its true sense. 'Based on trust' means not for actual ownership. There are difference of opinions between legal scholars in this matter. One view says that the creditor, the grantee of fiduciary security or fiduciairus, has become the actual owner of the secured property with all the rights vested to an owner. Other view says that the fiduciairus, for the benefit of third party, is regarded as owner, where against the grantor of fiducia is regarded as pledgee not holding the secured property because the parties do not actually intend to transfer the ownership right of secured property.[256]

236. Both opinions described above have their own consequences. If one accepts the first view, it means the fiduciairus is the owner of secured property. It will also mean that the ownership right is independent and theoretically fiduciaries can transfer the secured property without transferring its receivable, even without considering

252. Sri Soedewi Masjchoen Sofwan, Mariam Darus Badrulzaman and D. Gandaprawira, as quoted by Rachmadi Usman, S.H., M.H., *Hukum Jaminan Keperdataan*, p. 150 (1st edition. Sinar Grafika 2008).
253. *Ibid.*, p. 174.
254. It is quoted from considerations of High Court of Surabaya dated 22 Mar. 1951 as set forth under H. 1952 Numbers 4 and 5, as quoted from J. Satrio, S.H., *Hukum Jaminan Hak Jaminan Kebendaan*, p. 174 (Citra Aditya Bakti 1996).
255. *Ibid.*, p. 175.
256. J. Satrio, S.H., *Hukum Jaminan Hak Jaminan Kebendaan*, p. 176 (Citra Aditya Bakti 1996).

personal right of the debtor. In contrast, the second view fiducia as it is seen as pledge without possession of the secured property, then the security agreement is accessory to the principal agreement. This means that transfer of receivable will mean that the secured property through fiducia will also be transferred.[257] Sri Soedewi Masjchoen Sofwan explains that a fiducia agreement does not result in full ownership of the creditor since the creditor does not possess the property, is not authorized to enjoy the property, and only has authority over the property related to the agreed intent, namely as security. If the debtor defaults, he can still use and possess the property, is able to defend it, also against the third party, namely against fiduciairus. Even the debtor is able to defend his right against the receiver if there is a bankruptcy of creditor.[258]

237. Other issues, if debtor defaults, will the creditor become the owner of the secured property (first view)? If the creditor will not become the actual owner of the secured property, does it mean that the secured property is still owned by the debtor? This question is not necessarily true since there is also a provision stipulating that the debtor will be considered as user or holder against the creditor as owner.[259]

238. Pitlo opines that the creditor has become the actual owner but with limited authority. The right of creditor against the secured property is limited to the obligatory agreement, since as an owner, the creditor is not allowed to sell, re-pledge, exchange, or use it. These limitations are tightly related to the intent of delivery of ownership right, which is as security right only. This means that the creditor is obligated to return it. Accordingly some interpret fiducia as delivery of ownership but with conditions.[260] This opinion is in conformance with the opinion that considers a fiducia agreement as obligatory agreement and causes personal rights, according to the system of Roman law, namely *fiducia cum creditoria*. Its classic meaning refers to the ownership right of the creditor, even though there are limitations as agreed by the parties, debtor and creditor. Similar opinion also emerged according to the development of Anglo-American based on common law, where the holder of mortgage is considered to have an ownership over secured property, becoming *eigenaar* of the secured property and is considered as title-holder.[261]

239. Fiduciary is a transfer of ownership of an object on trust with the provision that the transferred property remains in the control of the owner of the object. Fiduciary security is defined as the right over movable property both tangible and intangible and immovable property, particularly buildings that cannot be burdened with mortgaged as set forth under Mortgage Law which remain in control of the grantor of the fiduciary

257. *Ibid.*, p. 177.
258. Sri Soedewi Masjchoen Sofwan as quoted by Rachmadi Usman, S.H., M.H., *Hukum Jaminan Keperdataan*, p. 163 (1st edition. Sinar Grafika 2008).
259. Article 18 suc 3c of Loan Agreement BNI'46 Model P.K.1 as quoted from J. Satrio, S.H., *Hukum Jaminan Hak Jaminan Kebendaan*, p. 178 (Citra Aditya Bakti 1996).
260. Mr Sumardi Mangunkusumo, *Suatu Tinjauan Mengenai Sistematika Jaminan Yang Diharuskan oleh Pasal 24 U.U Perbankan No. 14/1967 Bagi Pemberian Kredit oleh Bank Umum*, Seminar Hukum Jaminan, p. 1977, as quoted from J. Satrio, S.H., *Hukum Jaminan Hak Jaminan Kebendaan*, p. 178 (Citra Aditya Bakti 1996).
261. Sri Soedewi Masjchoen Sofwan as quoted by Rachmadi Usman, S.H., M.H., *Hukum Jaminan Keperdataan*, p. 163 (1st edition. Sinar Grafika 2008).

security, as collateral for the repayment of certain loan, which gives priority to the fiduciairus or grantee of fiduciary security against other creditors.[262]

240. Fiduciary Security Law is not applicable to mortgage right related to land and building, to the extent the prevailing laws and regulations determined that those properties must be registered. This also means that the building built over other people's land which cannot be mortgaged can be secured through a fiduciary security. Further, it is not applicable to hypothec over registered ship with gross volume of 20 cubic metre or more, hypothec of aircraft, and pledge.[263] J. Satrio considers this provision is exaggerated and unnecessary since by itself provisions of Fiduciary Security Law are not applicable if the secured property is subject to other law, such as Mortgage Law, pledge, or hypothec.[264]

241. Accordingly, properties that can be secured through a fiduciary security are:

(1) Movable tangible property.
(2) Movable intangible property, such as receivable.
(3) Registered movable property.
(4) Unregistered movable property.
(5) Certain immovable property that is unable to be mortgaged under Mortgage Law.
(6) Certain immovable property, that is unable to be secured through hypothec.
(7) A property that can be owned and transferred.[265]

242. A fiduciary security is an accessory agreement to its principal agreement that creates any obligation for the parties to perform. The meaning of 'perform' or 'performance' includes giving something, doing something, or not doing something, which can be valued with money.[266]

243. Pledge of a fiduciary over a property is made by a notarial deed in the Indonesian language and is meant as deed of fiduciary security. In the deed, in addition to the stipulation of date, the time (hour) must also be included.[267]

244. A deed of fiduciary security shall at least contain the following:[268]

(1) Identity of the giver and receiver of the fiducia; The term 'identity' includes the full name, religion, residence, or domicile, place and date of birth, gender, marital status, and employment.
(2) Information on the principal agreement secured by the fiducia; a description includes the type of agreement and debt secured by the fiducia.

262. Article 1 point 2 of Fiducia Law.
263. Article 3 of Fiducia Law.
264. J. Satrio as quoted from Rachmadi Usman, S.H., M.H., *Hukum Jaminan Keperdataan*, p. 178 (1st edition. Sinar Grafika 2008).
265. Rachmadi Usman, S.H., M.H., *Hukum Jaminan Keperdataan*, p. 177 (1st edition. Sinar Grafika 2008).
266. Article 4 of Fiducia Law.
267. Article 5 para. (1) of Fiducia Law.
268. Article 6 of Fiducia Law.

(3) Description of the property of the fiducia; a description is made by identifying the property and explaining its ownership document. If the property of fiducia is an inventory that are always altered or not permanent, such as stock of raw materials, finished property, or a portfolio of securities, the deed of fiduciary security includes the description of the type, brand, quality of the property.
(4) Value of the guarantee.
(5) Value of the object of the fiducia.

245. The requirements to mention those information in the deed of fiduciary security is related to the specialty principle adopted by the Fiduciary Security Law, and eventually supporting the principle of legal certaintyis one of the goals of the Fiduciary Security Law.[269]

246. Debt repayment secured by the fiducia can be:

(1) an existing debt;
(2) debt that will arise in the future which has been agreed in a certain amount; this is known as 'contingent', for example, debt arising from payment made by the creditor for the benefit of debtor in the context of bank guarantee; and
(3) debt that can be quantified at the time of execution of the principal agreement creating obligation to perform; this provision refers to the owed interest on the principal loan amount and other costs to be determined later.[270]

247. Debt that can be secured by fiducia is not limited to the meaning of debt under Fiduciary Security Law, but also includes any agreements as stipulated under Articles 1233 and 1234 of ICC.[271] It means that any type of agreements can be secured by the fiduciary security.

248. Nowadays, the entrepreneurs drawing loan from the bank through a checking account with a purpose to save as much as possible the interest payment. It is highly rare that entrepreneur draws a loan that its amount would be certain from the beginning (fix loan). Under a checking account loan, bank can only determine a loan plafond that serves as maximum amount a debtor may withdraw. Since normally debtor's flow of fund – to save interest – is conducted through debtor's bank account at the creditor's bank, the amount of money that is actually indebted by the debtor can vary from time to time.[272] Since debtor's debt – according to the agreement – may vary and fiduciary security may be useful when the creditor, due to debtor's breach of contract, will execute the secured property, then the indebted amount by the debtor is important and must be known for sure when the execution is performed. Accordingly, the provision under the Fiduciary Security Law as described above assists the necessity of the banking

269. J. Satrio as quoted by Rachmadi Usman, S.H., M.H., *Hukum Jaminan Keperdataan*, p. 193 (1st edition. Sinar Grafika 2008).
270. Article 7 of Fiducia Law.
271. Fred B.G. Tumbuan as quoted by Rachmadi Usman, S.H., M.H., *Hukum Jaminan Keperdataan*, p. 183 (1st edition. Sinar Grafika 2008).
272. J. Satrio as quoted by Rachmadi Usman, S.H., M.H., *Hukum Jaminan Keperdataan*, p. 182 (1st edition. Sinar Grafika 2008).

world. What is important, at the time of execution, is that the indebted amount can be determined.[273]

249. A fiduciary security can be granted to more than one recipient or through a power of attorney or a representative of the recipient of fiducia. This provision is applicable if the creditors are consortium providing loans. Since the fiduciary security will immediately be registered, it can be concluded that the granting of fiduciary security to more than one creditor can only be made within one deed of granting of fiduciary security. Even though there are many creditors, the fiduciary security is granted once for all within the same deed to all their creditors.[274] 'Power of attorney' is given to the person who has special power of recipient of fiducia to represent their interest in the acceptance of fiducia from the grantor. 'Representative' is a person who is legally considered to represent the fiducia for fiduciary security acceptance, for example, the trustee in representing the interest of bondholders.[275]

250. Fiduciary security can be granted against one or more units or types of property, including account receivable, whether existing at the time the guarantee is given or acquired later. Its fiducia pledge does not have to be made in a separate agreement. This provision is crucially important from the commercial perspective. This provision strictly allows a fiduciary security to include property that will be obtained in the future. This demonstrates flexibility of law with regard to the objects that can be secured by fiducia for the repayment of debt.[276]

251. Unless agreed otherwise:

(1) Fiduciary security includes proceeds of secured property; The meaning of 'proceeds of the secured property' is anything derived from the secured property of fiduciary security.
(2) Fiduciary security includes insurance claim, if the secured property is insured; this provision emphasizes that insurance claim is the right of recipient of fiduciary security.[277]

252. Property secured with fiduciary security must be registered.[278] If the property is outside territory of the Republic of Indonesia, the obligation to register the secured property is in effect.[279] The registration of property secured with fiduciary security is conducted at the domicile of the grantor, and registration includes object, both inside and outside the territory of the Republic of Indonesia to fulfil the principle of publicity, and as assurance against other creditors of the property with regards to the properties secured with the fiduciary security.[280]

273. J. Satrio as quoted from Rachmadi Usman, S.H., M.H., *Hukum Jaminan Keperdataan*, p. 183 (1st edition. Sinar Grafika 2008).
274. J. Satrio as quoted from Rachmadi Usman, S.H., M.H., *Hukum Jaminan Keperdataan*, p. 184 (1st edition. Sinar Grafika 2008).
275. Article 8 and its elucidation of Fiducia Law.
276. Article 8 and its elucidation of Fiducia Law.
277. Article 10 and its elucidation of Fiducia Law.
278. Article 11 para. (1) of Fiducia Law.
279. Article 11 para. (2) of Fiducia Law.
280. Elucidation of Article 11 para. (2) of Fiducia Law.

253. Application for registration is made by the recipient of fiduciary security, his proxy or his representative by attaching the registration statement of fiduciary security.[281] The registration statement contains:[282]

(1) Identity of the grantor and recipient of fiduciary security.
(2) Date, number of the deed of fiduciary security, name, and domicile of notary preparing the deed.
(3) Information of principal agreement secured with fiduciary security.
(4) Description of the object of fiduciary security.
(5) Value of the guarantee.
(6) Value of the object of fiduciary security.

254. What is obligated to register is the 'fiduciary security bond', or can be read as, including the 'property' secured with the fiduciary security and altogether its 'bond', namely fiduciary security. Provisions of Fiduciary Security Law show that what is required to register is the 'bond' of fiduciary security, and therefore, the product issued by the fiducia registration office is called as 'certificate of fiduciary security' not 'certificate of property of fiduciary security'.[283]

255. The fiducia registration office inserts the fiduciary security into the book of fiducia register on the same date as the receipt date of application.[284] This provision is intended so that the fiducia registration office does not conduct an assessment of the truthfulness contained in the registration statement of the fiduciary security, but only examining the data as it should have been contained in the registration statement.[285] That information is open for public.[286] Making the information open for public refers to the specialty and publicity principles. It is intended for third party so that the third party is bound for its registration where the third party is unable to defend his negligence by reason of having conducted his actions in good faith with regards to the secured property.[287]

256. The fiducia registration office will then issue and deliver to the recipient of fiduciary security a certificate of fiduciary security on the same date with the receipt date of registration application. Certificate of fiduciary security is a copy of book of fiducia register containing records as mentioned in the application. The fiduciary security comes into existence on the same date as the registration date of fiduciary security in the book of fiducia register. This provision is without prejudice to the applicability of the delivery of registered receivables and other intangible property as set forth in Article 613 of ICC.[288] The time of existence of fiduciary security is different

281. Article 13 para. (1) of Fiducia Law.
282. Article 13 para. (2) of Fiducia Law.
283. Rachmadi Usman, S.H., M.H., *Hukum Jaminan Keperdataan*, p. 202 (1st edition. Sinar Grafika 2008).
284. Article 13 para. (3) of Fiducia Law.
285. Elucidation of Art. 13 para. (3) of Fiducia Law.
286. Article 18 of Fiducia Law.
287. J. Satrio as quoted by Rachmadi Usman, S.H., M.H., *Hukum Jaminan Keperdataan*, p. 207 (1st edition. Sinar Grafika 2008).
288. Article 14 and its elucidation of Fiducia Law.

than the customary law stating that a transaction is clear, which means that it is made before the public official and cash. Accordingly, under customary law, the fiducia should have been come into existence at the time the deed of fiduciary security before the public official is made.[289]

257. The certificate of fiduciary security contains wordings 'FOR THE SAKE OF JUSTICE UNDER ONE ALMIGHTY GOD'. This certificate has the same execution power as the court's decision that is final and binding. This also means that the when the debtor defaults, the creditor can immediately execute the fiduciary security without involvement of court, by way of selling the secured property based on his sole discretion.[290] Since the certificate of fiduciary security is issued by authorized institution, in this matter a fiducia registration office, then a certificate of fiduciary security has a strong evidentiary power as an authentic deed and only the fiducia registration office that is able to issue it. Therefore, all other types of evidences in any forms whatsoever should be declined.[291]

258. Grantor of fiduciary security is prohibited from re-encumbering the property that is secured with the registered fiduciary security. This provision emphasizes that re-encumbering is not possible since the right of ownership over property has been assigned to the recipient of fiduciary security.[292]

259. The transfer of underlying receivables that are secured with fiduciary security causes the transfer by virtue of law all rights and obligations of the recipient of fiduciary security to the new creditor. This transfer is registered by the new creditor through the fiduciary security registration office. The transfer of receivable, also known as 'cessie', is the transfer of receivable by way of an authentic or privately drawn deed. Through this cessie, all rights and obligations of the previous recipient of fiduciary security is transferred to the new recipient of fiduciary security and its transfer is notified to the grantor of fiduciary security.[293] This provision is essentially referred to in Article 613 of ICC.

260. One has to be watchful, however, that there are two transfers, first, transfer of 'receivable' and second, transfer of 'security'. This transfer is different than the transfer of pledge, hypothec, and mortgage right, where due to the transfer of principal agreement from previous creditor to the new creditor it automatically is transferred then to the new creditor. On pledge, hypothec, and mortgage right, there is no issue on transfer of 'ownership'. In fiducia, there is an issue of transfer of 'ownership'. Since fiducia is accessory to its principal agreement, then the transfer of that agreement causes that by virtue of law, the fiduciary security is also transferred following its principal agreement. Its logical consequence, 'ownership' over property secured with fiduciary security, is transferred from previous creditor to the new creditor, where there are to delivery of ownership from previous creditor to the new creditor. This means that there is an alternative way to transfer a property, namely without delivery. This

289. Munir Fuady as quoted by Rachmadi Usman, S.H., M.H., *Hukum Jaminan Keperdataan*, p. 212 (1st edition. Sinar Grafika 2008).
290. Article 15 and its elucidation of Fiducia Law.
291. Munir Fuady as quoted by Rachmadi Usman, S.H., M.H., *Hukum Jaminan Keperdataan*, p. 214 (1st edition. Sinar Grafika 2008).
292. Article 17 of Fiducia Law.
293. Article 19 of Fiducia Law.

is logical but it is better if the new creditor requests to the previous creditor that the 'ownership' of property secured with the fiduciary security is also transferred.[294]

261. Fiduciary security is terminated due to the following:

(1) abolition of the debt secured by the fiducia; abolition includes repayment and evidence of void of debt through a letter issued by the creditor. This provision is interpreted broadly, including all agreements, since in principle, this security institution can be used to secure all performances arising from any agreements;[295]
(2) release by the recipient of the fiducia; or
(3) devastation of the property secured with fiducia, according to the principles of fiduciary security, the existence of fiducia depends on the existence of a secured receivable. If the receivable is void as a result of abolition or release, then by itself, the fiduciary security will be terminated.[296]

262. If the property secured by fiduciary security is devastated, it will not eliminate the insurance claim. The insurance claim will serve as substitute of the fiduciary security object.[297] The recipient of fiduciary security will notify the fiducia registration office about the termination of fiduciary security by attaching a statement on repayment of debt, release of right, or devastation of property secured with the fiduciary security.[298] The fiducia registration office will delete the record of fiduciary security from the book of fiducia register and will issue an information letter stating that certificate of fiduciary security is no longer valid.[299]

263. As per other property right, recipient of fiduciary security is considered as having preferential right. This preference is commenced since registration date of property is secured with fiduciary security by the fiducia registration office. The preference right means that the recipient of fiduciary security is entitled to obtain repayment of receivable by executing the secured property. This right will not be terminated as a result of bankruptcy and/or liquidation by the grantor of fiduciary security.[300] Bankruptcy Law stipulates that creditors holding pledge, fiduciary security, mortgage right, hypothec, or any other form of property right can execute their rights as if there is no bankruptcy.[301]

264. If the debtor or grantor of fiduciary security defaults, the execution of secured property can be conducted by:

(1) implementation of execution title by the recipient of fiduciary security;

294. J. Satrio as quoted by Rachmadi Usman, S.H., M.H., *Hukum Jaminan Keperdataan*, p. 219 (1st edition. Sinar Grafika 2008).
295. J. Satrio as quoted by Rachmadi Usman, S.H., M.H., *Hukum Jaminan Keperdataan*, p. 225 (1st edition. Sinar Grafika 2008).
296. Article 25 para. (1) and its elucidation of Fiducia Law.
297. Article 25 para. (2) and its elucidation of Fiducia Law.
298. Article 25 para. (3) of Fiducia Law.
299. Article 26 of Fiducia Law.
300. Article 27 and its elucidation of Fiducia Law.
301. Article 56 para. (1) of Bankruptcy Law.

(2) sale of secured property through public auction and obtain repayment of debt from its proceeds;
(3) sale privately based on agreement between the grantor of fiduciary security and recipient of fiduciary security if by doing that means, the highest price profitable for both parties can be achieved; specifically for the private sale, it can only be conducted after the lapse of one month after notified in writing by the grantor and or recipient of fiduciary security to other interested parties and has been announced at least in two newspapers within that region.[302]

If the secured property consists of tradeable properties or securities that can be sold through a market or stock exchange, their sale can be made at those places according to the prevailing laws and regulations.[303]

265. Fiduciary Security Law emphasizes that any covenant to execute the secured property by means of violating the above provision will be null and void.[304] If there is any covenant that the secured property will be owned by the creditor if the debtor defaults, it will be null and void.[305] These two provisions are the essential provisions for all types of security rights. Fiduciary Security Law also emphasizes that what will be annulled is not the principal agreement or its security agreement, but the provision specifying either the creditor will become the owner of the secured property or creditor can execute the secured property through other means set out under Fiduciary Security Law. This means, even though this type of provision exists in the principal agreement and/or security agreement, it will not be applicable.

266. It is also noteworthy that the entitlement to execute the secured property is conditional, which is only effective if the condition is fulfilled, namely, that the 'debtor or grantor of fiducia security defaults'. This provision differentiates between debtor and grantor of fiduciary security which in fact may be different. The word 'or' explains that either the debtor or grantor may be in default. Accordingly, one must differentiate default by debtor (when the debtor is the grantor of fiduciary security) and third party acting as grantor of fiduciary security. If the debtor is the grantor, there are two agreements that were executed, namely the principal agreement and deed of fiduciary security. Since the provision does not specify which agreement that may be defaulted, it means that the default includes the principal agreement and the security agreement. It is normal to regulate under the principal agreement, when the debtor defaults his covenants under any executed agreements, the debt will be due and payable.[306]

267. Grantor of fiduciary security shall deliver the secured property for the execution of the fiduciary security. If the grantor of fiduciary security does not surrender the secured property at the time of execution, the recipient of fiduciary security is entitled to take over the secured property and if necessary to request assistance from

302. Article 29 of Fiducia Law.
303. Article 31 of Fiducia Law.
304. Article 32 of Fiducia Law.
305. Article 33 of Fiducia Law.
306. J. Satrio as quoted by Rachmadi Usman, S.H., M.H., *Hukum Jaminan Keperdataan*, p. 231 (1st edition. Sinar Grafika 2008).

the authorities.[307] This provision gives assurance and protection to the creditor when the debtor is not cooperative with the creditor, when the creditor intends to execute the secured property. But in contrast, what may not be feasible to the creditor is the timing of the surrender of secured property. The longer the creditor has to wait for the debtor, the riskier it will be. During the wait period, until the secured property is surrendered to the creditor, the value of the secured property may be decreased and by the time of execution, its value may not be able to repay the debt.

268. Mortgage Law does not have stipulations on criminal provisions, but Fiducia Law has. One important criminal provision is that if the debtor transfers, pledges, or leases the secured property without any prior written consent of the recipient of fiduciary security, he will be sentenced with imprisonment the longest for two years and fine of Rp 50 million the most.[308]

307. Article 30 and its elucidation of Fiducia Law.
308. Article 36 of Fiducia Law.

Part V. Security

Chapter 1. Securities in Immovable Property (see also Parts I and IV)

§1. Privileges, Liens, Charges

269. ICC stipulates that all movable and immovable properties of the debtor, either present or future, serve as securities for the personal obligations of the debtor.[309] The properties serve as joint security for his creditors; the proceeds thereof are to be divided among the creditor in proportion to their loan, unless there exists a legal order of priority among the creditors.[310] These two provisions are the essential provisions of all security-related provisions under the laws and regulations.

270. The seniority among creditors shall be based upon privilege, pledge, and mortgage.[311]

271. Privilege is a right acknowledged by the law applicable to one creditor over the other, based upon the nature of the debt. Pledge and mortgage are superior to privilege, with the exception of the circumstances the law expressly stipulates otherwise.[312] The order of priority between creditors is regulated in accordance with the different nature of the priorities.[313] Creditors having the same priority shall be paid equally.[314]

272. The priority of the State's treasury, the auction offices, and other public institutions stipulated by high authority, the order in which they are be implemented, and the time of the duration, are regulated by the relevant legal ordinances. Associations or entities, which would have been authorized to or are further authorized to impose charges, are regulated by the ordinances already existing or to be further regulated.[315]

309. Article 1131 of ICC.
310. Article 1132 of ICC.
311. Article 1133 of ICC.
312. Article 1134 of ICC.
313. Article 1135 of ICC.
314. Article 1136 of ICC.
315. Article 1137 of ICC.

273. The subject of the priorities may be specific assets or all movable and immovable assets in general. The specific assets have priority over the latter mentioned.[316]

274. The priority of debts in respect of certain specific assets is as follows:

(1) The rent from immovable assets, the costs incurred in the repairs for which the lessee is responsible, including anything related to the compliance with the provisions of the lease agreement.
(2) Any amount due to bricklayers, carpenters, and other workmen as a result of the renovation, addition to and repairs of immovable assets, including a debt which is in existence for not more than three years, and the title to a plot which has been held by the debtor.

§2. Mortgage

275. In its consideration section, Mortgage Law states several reasons on the promulgation of Mortgage Law. Stipulation on hypothec as regulated in Book II of ICC as far as land is concerned, and the stipulation on *Credietverband* in *Staatsblad* 1908 Number 542 as already amended by *Staatsblad* 1937 Number 190, which pursuant to Article 57 of Agrarian Law, is temporarily applicable until the enactment of law on encumbrance, are deemed to be no longer compatible with the necessity of credit activities in relation to the development of Indonesia's economy.[317] Mortgage Law also views that it is necessary to establish a law which shall regulate mortgage right on land and land-related objects, as set forth in the Agrarian Law, and also concurrently unifying the national land law.[318]

276. There are several principles of Mortgage Law. First principle is that mortgage right gives preferential position to its creditor.[319] It means that, if debtor is in default, the creditor as the holder of Mortgage Right is entitled to sell in a public auction the land secured in accordance with the relevant laws and regulations, with the priority right over other creditors. Such priority right shall obviously not diminish the preference of the State's receivables under the prevailing laws and regulations.[320] This provision is in line with the current Tax Procedure Law.[321] State has preferential right for tax debt over taxpayer's property. Tax debt includes tax principal, administrative sanctions such as interest, penalties, increase, and tax collection expenses. The preferential right exceeds other preferential rights, except for court expenses caused by a decision to auction a movable and/or immovable property, expenses spent to save the property,

316. Article 1138 of ICC.
317. Consideration letter (c) of Mortgage Law.
318. Consideration letter (e) of Mortgage Law.
319. Prof. Dr St. Remy Sjahdeini, S.H., *Hak Tanggungan: Asas-Asas, Ketentuan-Ketentuan Pokok dan Masalah Yang Dihadapi Oleh Perbankan*, p. 15 (Alumni 1999).
320. General Elucidation point 4 of Mortgage Law.
321. Law Number 6 of 1983 on General Provisions and Tax Procedures as lastly amended by Law Number 16 of 2009 on Determination of Government Regulation in lieu of Law Number 5 of 2008 on Fourth Amendment to Law Number 6 of 1983 on General Provisions and Tax Procedures to become Law.

and/or court expenses. If the taxpayer is bankrupt, dissolved, or liquidated, then a receiver, liquidator, or individual or entity doing the administration is prohibited to distribute bankrupt debtor, dissolution or liquidation to shareholder or other creditor prior to using that asset to settle debtor's tax debt.[322]

277. Second principle says that mortgage right is undivided.[323] It means that mortgage right charges the object wholly and any part of it. If part of loan is repaid, it does not mean that part of mortgage object will be released. The mortgage right is still attached all objects of mortgage for the remaining loan that has not been repaid. This principle also means that partial deletion (*roya parsial*) is not possible.

278. Third principle says that it can only be charged over a definite land right.[324] Authority to take legal action over mortgage right object must be vested at the grantor of mortgage right when registration of mortgage right is made.[325] A land right that will be owned in the future cannot be mortgaged for a certain repayment of loan. In other words, a charge of mortgage rights over land right that will be existed is not possible.

279. Fourth principle says that mortgage right can be pledged not only over land, but also over properties related to the land.[326] Properties include plants, buildings, and creations that are integral to the land. Properties related to the land are not limited to properties owned by the land owner but also properties owned by third parties.[327]

280. Fifth principle says that mortgage right can be secured over properties that will exist in the future.[328] Term of 'will exist' refers to properties, that at the time of mortgage right is made, are not yet existed. For example, those properties are just started, or planted, and not yet completed when the mortgage right is made. ICC is different than Mortgage Law in this regard. ICC contains accession principle, which means that without any agreement, any properties over the land will be automatically pledged through a hypothec. Mortgage Law derives from customary law which has different legal principle. Therefore, any properties over or related to land must be agreed in writing, if those properties are to be pledged under the mortgage right.

281. Mortgage right agreement is an accessory agreement.[329] A mortgage right agreement is not an independent agreement. Its existence is as a result of the existence of its parent agreement, namely loan agreement. Due to its nature as an accessory to certain receivable based on a loan agreement or any other agreement[330], the constitution and the existence of mortgage right would depend on the existence of the secured receivable.[331]

322. Article 21 paras (1), (2), (3) and (3a) of Tax Procedure Law.
323. Prof. Dr St. Remy Sjahdeini, S.H., *Hak Tanggungan: Asas-Asas, Ketentuan-Ketentuan Pokok dan Masalah Yang Dihadapi Oleh Perbankan*, p. 21 (Alumni 1999).
324. *Ibid.*, p. 25.
325. Article 8 para. (2) of Mortgage Law.
326. *Ibid.*, p. 26.
327. Article 4 paras (4) and (5) of Mortgage Law.
328. *Ibid.*, p. 27.
329. *Ibid.*, p. 28.
330. This also means that any other agreement without title of 'loan agreement' but creates an obligation to perform or to do something can be regarded as 'loan agreement'. *See* Art. 3 para. (1) of Mortgage Law.
331. Point 8 of General elucidation of Mortgage Law.

282. Seventh principle says that mortgage right can be made for new loan.[332] Payment obligation secured by mortgage right may be a debt which already exists, or has been agreed over a certain amount, or is in an amount determined upon application for the execution of the mortgage right under a loan agreement or an agreement giving rise to the indebtedness relationship.[333] A debt secured by mortgage right may be in the form of an existing loan as well as a debt not yet in existence but has been agreed upon, such as a debt arising from the payment by creditor in favour of debtor in the implementation of bank guarantee. The amount can be firmly stipulated in the agreement and can also afterwards be determined based on the calculation formula under the agreement which constitutes debt relationship, *inter alia*, interest rate of the principal loan, and other expenses incurred which figure of amount can only be firmly stipulated later.[334]

283. Eighth principle says that a mortgage right can secure more than one debt.[335] Mortgage right can be established to secure a debt originating from a legal relationship or for one or more debts originating from several legal relationships.[336] It frequently occurred that a debtor incurs debt to more than one creditor, each is based on a separate loan agreement, and for example the creditor is a bank and an affiliate of the bank. Receivable is secured by one mortgage right in favour of all creditors stated in the deed of granting of mortgage right. The mortgage right is established on the same plot of land. The relationship among creditors shall be agreed upon by themselves, while the creditors, in managing the relationship among creditors, the debtor and the grantor of mortgage right if the grantor is not a debtor, shall appoint one of the creditors who will act on behalf of themselves. The appointed creditor shall then appear before the PPAT to establish mortgage right, receive and possess the certificate of mortgage right.[337]

284. Ninth principle says that a mortgage right follows its object in whosoever hand it is located.[338] Accordingly, a mortgage right will not end even though its object is transferred to other party for whatsoever reasons. Under this principle, a holder of mortgage right will always be able to execute its rights even though the property is transferred. This is a manifestation of a '*droit de suite*' or '*zaakgevolg*' principle.[339] This principle is also taken over from hypothec principle that is regulated under ICC.[340]

285. Tenth principle says that a mortgage right can be encumbered with a seizure by the court. It is sure that a mortgage right is unable to be encumbered with seizure. This is because the intent of this security institution is to give strong security to the creditor holding a mortgage right to be prioritized among other creditors. If the court

332. Prof. Dr St. Remy Sjahdeini, S.H., *Hak Tanggungan: Asas-Asas, Ketentuan-Ketentuan Pokok dan Masalah Yang Dihadapi Oleh Perbankan*, p. 29 (Alumni 1999).
333. Article 3 para. (1) of Mortgage Law.
334. Elucidation of Art. 3 para. (1) of Mortgage Law.
335. *Ibid.*, p. 34.
336. Article 3 para. (2) of Mortgage Law.
337. Elucidation of Art. 3 para. (2) of Mortgage Law.
338. *Ibid.*, p. 38.
339. Prof. Dr St. Remy Sjahdeini, S.H., *Hak Tanggungan: Asas-Asas, Ketentuan-Ketentuan Pokok dan Masalah Yang Dihadapi Oleh Perbankan*, p. 39 (Alumni 1999).
340. The principle is regulated in Art. 1163 para. (2) and Art. 1198 of ICC.

puts on seizure, it means that the court disregards and waives the priority legal position of the creditor holding the mortgage right. A Supreme Court Decision Number 394 K/Pdt/1984 dated 31 May 1985 sets that properties that are pledged to secure a debt are security over loan by the Bank Rakyat Indonesia Cabang (Gresik), and hence unable to be seized.[341]

286. Eleventh principle says that a mortgage right can only be pledged to a certain land right. This principle is also called as specialty principle.[342] A deed of granting a mortgage right shall mention among others a clear description of the object of mortgage right.[343] Clear description on the mortgage right object must include specification of the relevant land title certificate, or for an unregistered land (uncertificated), at least the description of ownership, location, boundaries, and the area of the land.[344]

287. Twelfth principle says that a mortgage right must be registered.[345] A publicity principle is applicable to mortgage right. Registration of mortgage right constitutes absolute prerequisites for the creation of mortgage right and binding authority against a third party.[346] Registration also means the formation of book of land for mortgage right. The completion of the book of land for mortgage right fulfils the publicity principle and is binding to third party.[347]

288. Thirteenth principle says that a mortgage right can be granted with certain covenants.[348] Covenants included in the deed of granting of mortgage right are optional and do not affect the validity of the deed. The parties are free to determine whether to mention or not these covenants in the deed of granting of mortgage right. By containing those covenants in the deed of granting of mortgage right which is then registered with the land office, those covenants shall bind the third parties.[349] Those covenants are:[350]

(1) A covenant which restricts the authority of the grantor of mortgage right to lease the mortgage right object and/or determine or change the lease period and/or receive any lease payment in advance, unless there is a prior written approval from the holder of mortgage right; This covenant under hypothec regulation is called as *huurbeding*. Holder of hypothec may request that a covenant is made in the hypothec agreement that limits the grantor of hypothec if the grantor will lease the property that is pledged by hypothec. This covenant may be enforced upon the lessee/debtor by the creditor who has registered such covenant in the public register.[351] There is also another legal principle related to this covenant, which says that a sale and purchase agreement does not terminate lease agreement or in Dutch is also called as '*Koop breekt geen huur*'. It means that a property

341. *Ibid.*, p. 40.
342. *Ibid.*, p. 42. A similar provision is also regulated under Art. 1174 of ICC.
343. Article 11 para. (1) (e) of Mortgage Law.
344. Elucidation of Art. 11 para. (1) (e) of Mortgage Law.
345. *Ibid.*, p. 43.
346. Article 13 para. (1) of Mortgage Law.
347. Elucidation of Art. 13 para. (5) of Mortgage Law.
348. *Ibid.*, p. 44.
349. Elucidation of Art. 11 para. (2) of Mortgage Law.
350. Article 11 para. (2) of Mortgage Law.
351. Article 1185 of ICC.

under a lease agreement, if the property is sold by the owner to the third party, the lease agreement does not terminate as a result of that sale and purchase agreement. The buyer of property will replace the legal position as the lessor and is bound to the terms and conditions of the lease agreement.[352]

(2) A covenant which restricts the authority of a grantor of mortgage right to change the form or the arrangement of the mortgage right object, unless there is a prior written approval from the holder of mortgage right; a covenant to limit the alteration of form or shape of mortgage right is required by the creditor to prevent the value of mortgage right object to be decreased as a consequence of that alteration. An agreement can be made that an alteration is possible provided that it has obtained prior approval in writing from the creditor.[353]

(3) A covenant conferring authority to a holder of mortgage right to manage the mortgage right object pursuant to decision of the head of district court having jurisdiction over the mortgage right object if the debtor is in default; a covenant which authorizes the holder of mortgage right to manage the mortgage right object may inflict financial loss to the grantor of mortgage right. Accordingly, such covenant shall be supported with a prerequisite that the decision of the Chairman of District Court is required for the execution. Prior to the issuance of such decision, the Chairman of District Court shall summon and conduct hearing from the relevant parties, consisting of the holder of mortgage right and the grantor of mortgage right and the debtor if the grantor of mortgage right is not the debtor.[354]

(4) A covenant conferring authority to holder of mortgage right to save the mortgage right object, if this is necessary for the implementation of an execution or to prevent the waiver or cancellation of the right over the mortgage right object because of non-fulfilment of or violations of laws; This covenant includes the delegation authority to the holder of mortgage right at the expense of the grantor of mortgage right object to avoid the annulment of mortgage right due to the land title being null and void, and to conduct any other work necessary to prevent value deterioration of the mortgage right object resulting in the lower selling price, so that it may not be sufficient to cover the secured debt in full.[355] An event of removal or cancellation of land right which is pledged by mortgage right will also terminate the mortgage right. This will cause huge losses to the holder of mortgage right if the debtor or grantor or mortgage right does not conduct necessary actions to rescue the land right pledged with a mortgage right.[356]

(5) A covenant that the holder of first mortgage right be entitled to sell by virtue of his own authority the mortgage right object if the debtor is in default; This covenant conforms to the right of creditor, if the debtor is in default, to sell based on his own authority the mortgage right object in a public auction and collect the sales

352. Prof. Dr St. Remy Sjahdeini, S.H., *Hak Tanggungan: Asas-Asas, Ketentuan-Ketentuan Pokok dan Masalah Yang Dihadapi Oleh Perbankan*, pp. 81–82 (Alumni 1999).
353. *Ibid.*, pp. 84–85.
354. Elucidation of Art. 11 para. (2) (c) of Mortgage Law.
355. Elucidation of Art. 11 para. (2) (d) of Mortgage Law.
356. Prof. Dr St. Remy Sjahdeini, S.H., *Hak Tanggungan: Asas-Asas, Ketentuan-Ketentuan Pokok dan Masalah Yang Dihadapi Oleh Perbankan*, p. 88 (Alumni 1999).

proceeds to recover the receivables.[357] This covenant is essentially not necessary. The insertion of this covenant or its non-insertion does not affect entitlement of the creditor to execute his mortgage right under the Mortgage Law.

(6) A covenant given by the holder of first mortgage right that the mortgage right object shall not be disposed from mortgage right; This covenant is intended to protect the interest of the second-ranked holder of mortgage right and its successor. By virtue of this covenants, without any approval to write off given by the second-ranked holder of mortgage right and its successors, the second-ranked holder of mortgage right object through the object has been executed to pay the debt of the first-ranked holder of mortgage right.[358] This covenant should have been given in reverse. The covenant should be given from the grantor of mortgage right to the first-ranked holder of mortgage right, not vice versa as stipulated under Mortgage Law.[359] Hence, the covenant should be stated, '*a covenant granted by the grantor of mortgage right to the first-ranked holder of mortgage right that the mortgage right object is unable to be removed from the mortgage right*'.[360]

(7) A covenant that the grantor of mortgage right shall not release his right over the mortgage right object without a prior written approval from the holder of mortgage right; The removal of land right can occur by means of voluntary relinquishment by the grantor of mortgage right. To protect the creditor/holder of mortgage right, a covenant that the debtor or landowner will not do voluntary relinquishment is important.[361]

(8) A covenant that the holder of mortgage right shall receive all or part of the compensation received by the grantor of mortgage right or the satisfaction of his receivables if the grantor of mortgage right releases his right over the object or mortgage right or if the right is revoked for public interest; It is possible that the relinquishment of land right pledged by mortgage right is intended to obtain compensation to repay the loan to the creditor. This means that it is not reasonable if the creditor does not approve the land right relinquishment. This covenant also means that if the relinquishment is made due to the public interest procurement, the debtor should make available the sales proceeds to the creditor to repay his debts.[362]

(9) A covenant that the holder of mortgage right shall receive all or part of the insurance proceeds received by the grantor of mortgage right for his receivables payment if the mortgage right is insured; This covenant is necessary for the creditor. In practice, this covenant is also inserted into the insurance policy for the mortgage right object. This clause is called as 'banker's clause'.[363]

(10) A covenant that the grantor of mortgage right shall vacate the mortgage right object upon the execution of mortgage right; This covenant is necessary to obtain

357. Article 6 of Mortgage Law.

358. Elucidation of Art. 11 para. (2) (f) of Mortgage Law.

359. *Ibid.*, pp. 92–93.

360. Prof. Dr St. Remy Sjahdeini, S.H., *Hak Tanggungan: Asas-Asas, Ketentuan-Ketentuan Pokok dan Masalah Yang Dihadapi Oleh Perbankan*, p. 93 (Alumni 1999).

361. *Ibid.*, p. 94.

362. *Ibid.*, pp. 95–96.

363. *Ibid.*, p. 97.

maximum selling price of the mortgage right object.[364]What is necessary, other than a covenant, is entitlement that the holder of mortgage right may request judgment or determination by the Chairman of District Court to order abandonment of the mortgage right object and to perform abandonment to anyone with the assistance of police if the tenants are not willing to leave voluntarily. If this is given to the creditor, this covenant will have meaning.[365]

(11) A covenant that the certificate of land right will be held by the holder of mortgage right until the debt is paid-off. Without the inclusion of this covenant, the certificate of land right pledged by mortgage right will still be held by the landowner.[366]

289. Fourteenth principle says that a covenant that authorizes the holder of mortgage right to own the mortgage object if the debtor is in default will become null and void.[367] This provision protects the interest of the debtor and the grantor of other mortgage right, especially when the value of the mortgage right object exceeds the amount of secured debt. But the holder of mortgage right may become the purchaser of the mortgage right object according to the prevailing procedure under the Mortgage Law.[368]

290. Fifteenth principle says that if the debtor is in default, the holder of the first mortgage right is entitled to sell mortgage right object based on its authority through public auction and recover the repayment as a result of the sale. This means that the holder of mortgage right is not required to obtain approval from the grantor of mortgage right or requesting for determination from the court. The holder of mortgage right can just visit the chairman of auction to auction the mortgage right object.[369]

291. A right to sell mortgage right object on his own authority is one manifestation of preference right of the holder of mortgage right or the holder of first-ranked mortgage right if there are more than one holder of mortgage right. Such right is based on the covenant given by the grantor of mortgage right that if the debtor fails to fulfil his promise, the holder of mortgage right is entitled to sell the mortgage right object in public auction without any other approval from the grantor of mortgage right, and the receivables will be collected from the sale proceeds prior to distribution for other creditors. The remaining sale proceeds will still belong to the grantor of mortgage right.[370]

292. Certificate of mortgage right serves as evidence that a mortgage right has been issued by a land office and contains wordings 'FOR THE SAKE OF JUSTICE BASED ON ALMIGTHY GOD' has the same executorial power as court decision that obtains a permanent legal power. Thus, the execution of mortgage right can be made without any civil claim proceeding if the debtor is in default. The certificate also serves as a substitute of Grosse deed of hypothec to the extent that it is for land right.[371]

364. Elucidation of Art. 11 para. (2) (j) of Mortgage Law.
365. *Ibid.*, p. 98.
366. Elucidation of Art. 11 para. (2) (k) of Mortgage Law.
367. *Ibid.*, p. 45.
368. Elucidation of Art. 12 of Mortgage Law.
369. *Ibid.*, p. 47.
370. Elucidation of Art. 6 of Mortgage Law.
371. Elucidation of Art. 14 para. (3) of Mortgage Law.

293. The granting of mortgage is preceded with a covenant to grant mortgage right as security for particular debt payment, contained in and forming inseparable part of a loan agreement or of another agreement giving rise to such debt.[372] This provision is in compliance to the accessory nature of mortgage right where the imposition shall follow the principal agreement, namely the secured agreement which results in the loan relationship. The agreement establishing loan relationship may be prepared using privately drawn deed or notarial deed. If the loan relationship arises from a loan agreement, such agreement may be made inside or outside of the country or the relevant parties concerned may be foreign individuals or foreign legal entities to the extent that the loans concerned is used for the development in the jurisdiction in Indonesia.[373] Briefly, the issuance of mortgage right is only possible if there is an agreement under the loan agreement that the debtor will grant a mortgage right to the creditor. The granting of mortgage right will then be made using a deed of granting a mortgage right by PPAT. This provision does not exist under hypothec regulation.[374]

294. The grantor of mortgage right may be an individual or a legal entity having the authority to do legal action against the mortgage right object.[375] Authority to take legal action against the mortgage right must have existed with the grantor at the time the mortgage right registration is made.[376] Since the mortgage right is born upon its registration, the authority to conduct legal action against the mortgage right object must be in the grantor upon the preparation of book of land for mortgage right. Accordingly, it has to be proven that the grantor's authority is legitimate at the time the mortgage right is registered.[377]

295. If the grantor of mortgage right is a limited liability company, implementation of grant must comply with the Company Law. Under Company Law, the Board of Directors is obligated to seek approval from the general meeting of shareholders to transfer company's property or pledge company's property, which constitutes more than 50% of company's net property within one transaction or more, whether or not they are related.[378] The quorum to seek approval by GMS is at least three-fourths of all shares with voting rights that are present and decided by at least three-fourths of all voting rights, unless company's articles of association determine higher requirement.[379]

296. The holder of mortgage right may be an individual or a legal entity being in a position as the party having receivables to be collected.[380]

297. There are requirements for the deed of granting a mortgage to be legitimate. If the deed does not mention what is required under the Mortgage Law, the deed will be null and void. The deed of granting a mortgage right shall mention:

---

372. Article 10 para. (1) of Mortgage Law.
373. Elucidation of Art. 10 para. (1) of Mortgage Law.
374. Prof. Dr St. Remy Sjahdeini, S.H., *Hak Tanggungan: Asas-Asas, Ketentuan-Ketentuan Pokok dan Masalah Yang Dihadapi Oleh Perbankan*, p. 50 (Alumni 1999).
375. Article 8 para. (1) of Mortgage Law.
376. Article 8 para. (2) of Mortgage Law.
377. Elucidation of Art. 8 para. (2) of Mortgage Law.
378. Article 102 para. (1) of Company Law.
379. Article 102 para. (5) of Company Law jo. Article 89 of Company Law.
380. Article 9 of Mortgage Law.

(1) Name and identity of the holder and the grantor of mortgage right; If the mortgage right is imposed upon land-related objects owned by a person or legal entity other than the holder of land title, both the holder of land title and jointly with the owner of the land-related objects shall act as the grantor of mortgage right.[381]
(2) Domicile of the parties, and if among them there may be a party domiciled outside Indonesia, a chosen domicile in Indonesia must also be mentioned in his favour, and if the chosen domicile is not mentioned, the office of the PPAT where the deed is drawn will be considered as the chosen domicile; By assuming PPAT's office as the legal domicile of a foreign party, it has fulfilled the prerequisite of chosen domicile.[382]
(3) Clear reference to the debt or debts secured; this information also includes name and identity of the debtor.[383]
(4) Value of the mortgage.
(5) Clear description of the mortgage right object.[384] Description will also include specification of the relevant land title certificate of, for an unregistered land, at least the description of ownership, location, boundaries, and the area of such land.[385]

298. A mortgage right object can be imposed with more than one mortgage right as security for the payment of more than one debts. This means that there will be first-ranked, second-ranked, and third-ranked holder of mortgage right.[386] The ranking of each mortgage right will be determined by the date of registration at the land office. This refers to the date of book of land of mortgage right.[387] If there are mortgage right registered on the same date, the rank will be determined by the date the deed of granting a mortgage is made. This provision refers to the serial number of the deed since the preparation of more than one deed can only be carried out by the same PPAT.[388]

299. Provision on using the same PPAT creates confusion. This provision is considered as ineffective and non-accommodative. This provision should have been stipulated under the provisions of the law, not in its elucidation. Questions arise, what will be the legal consequence, if the deed is made by other PPAT (not the same one as previous deed). Would the deed be null and void? Since elucidation is not a legal norm, this elucidation can be disregarded.[389]

300. Legal consequences of different rank holders of mortgage right are not regulated in the Mortgage Law. This means that hypothec regulation should be referred to. The holder of higher-ranked mortgage right, as per hypothec regulation, will be

381. Elucidation of Art. 11 para. (1) (a) of Mortgage Law.
382. Elucidation of Art. 11 para. (1) (b) of Mortgage Law.
383. Elucidation of Art. 11 para. (1) (c) of Mortgage Law.
384. Article 11 para. (1) of Mortgage Law.
385. Elucidation of Art. 11 para. (1) (e) of Mortgage Law.
386. Article 5 para. (1) of Mortgage Law and its elucidation.
387. Article 5 para. (2) of Mortgage Law and its elucidation.
388. Article 5 para. (3) of Mortgage Law and its elucidation.
389. Prof. Dr St. Remy Sjahdeini, S.H., *Hak Tanggungan: Asas-Asas, Ketentuan-Ketentuan Pokok dan Masalah Yang Dihadapi Oleh Perbankan*, pp. 124–125 (Alumni 1999).

prioritized from the lower-ranked holder of mortgage right, to obtain the repayment of public auction proceeds. Briefly, the first-ranked holder is prioritized over second-ranked holder, and the second-ranked holder is prioritized over the third-ranked holder of mortgage right.[390] It also means that from the proceeds from a public auction, the first-ranked shall be repaid first. If there is remaining money, the second-ranked shall be repaid, and the remaining fund will be for the third-ranked holder of mortgage right. If after all the holders are repaid and there is still remaining fund, it will be returned to the debtor.

301. If the receivables secured with mortgage right is transferred through cession,[391] subrogation,[392] inheritance, or other reasons[393], the mortgage right will also be transferred by law to the new creditor.[394] Since the transfer of mortgage right occurs by virtue of laws, such legal act does not have to be evidenced with deed of PPAT.[395] The transfer of mortgage right will be registered by the new creditor at the land office. The registration will be conducted by the land office by recording it in the book of land of mortgage right and the book of land for land title which becomes the object of mortgage right, and copying the same in the certificate of mortgage right and certificate of land right. The recording date in the book of land will be the date of seventh day after the receipt in full of the documents required for the registration on the transfer of mortgage right and if the seventh day falls on a public holiday, the recording date will be on the next business day.[396]

302. Acquisition does not change the legal entity of the company. What is changed is the owners or shareholders of the company. Accordingly, a company as creditor and owner of receivables does not change. There is no transfer of receivable in an acquisition of company.[397]

303. In a merger or consolidation, a company will take over all assets and liabilities of other company. In a merger,[398] receivables of the merged company is

---

390. *Ibid.*, p. 126.
391. Cession is a legal act of transferring receivables by a creditor as the holder of mortgage right to another party (Elucidation of Art. 16 para. (1) of Mortgage Law).
392. Subrogation is a replacement of a credit by a third party who pays debtor's debt (Elucidation of Art. 16 para. (1) of Mortgage Law).
393. The words 'any other reason' means anything other than cession and subrogation in the event of merger or acquisition so that to cause the transfer of receivable from the previous company to the new company (Elucidation of Art. 16 para. (1) of Mortgage Law).
394. Article 16 of Mortgage Law.
395. Elucidation of Art. 16 para. (1) of Mortgage Law.
396. Article 16 of Mortgage Law.
397. Prof. Dr St. Remy Sjahdeini, S.H., *Hak Tanggungan: Asas-Asas, Ketentuan-Ketentuan Pokok dan Masalah Yang Dihadapi Oleh Perbankan*, p. 129 (Alumni 1999).
398. Merger means a legal act conducted by one company or more to merge itself with other existing company that causes assets and liabilities of the merged company transferred by virtue of law to the company receiving the merger and consequently, the status of legal entity of merged company is terminated (Art. 1 point 9 of Company Law).

transferred to the company that is absorbing the merged company. In a consolidation,[399] receivables of both companies are transferred to a new company (third company). In merger and consolidation there is a transfer of receivables and creditor.[400]

304. Mortgage right is annulled due to the following:[401]

(1) The debt secured by mortgage right is void; since the existence of mortgage right depends on the existence of secured receivables, if the receivables is void or paid-off, the mortgage right shall also be void.[402]
(2) The holder of mortgage right releases the mortgage right; the mortgage right can be voluntarily released. The mortgage right can also be inoperative if the land right is released.[403] Nevertheless, even though the mortgage right is annulled due the annulment of land right, the loan that was previously made is still in existence.[404]
(3) Deletion of mortgage right under the judgment of ranking by the Chairman of District Court.
(4) The land title secured by mortgage right is void. The land title may be void to several reasons, *inter alia*, revocation of right, voluntary relinquishment by the owner, abandonment, violation of the requirement of holders of land right. Nevertheless, if the period of land right ends and extends based on the application prior to the expiry of its period, the mortgage right will still be attached to the related land right.[405]

305. The purchaser of the mortgage right object, either in public auction at the order of Chairman of District Court or on a voluntary transaction, may demand the holder of mortgage right that the mortgage right exceeding the purchase price over the object purchased be written off. This is to protect the interest of the buyers of mortgage right, to release the purchased real property from the mortgage right, if the purchase price is not sufficient to fulfil the secured debt.[406]

306. The release of mortgage right object shall be made through a written statement from the holder of mortgage right containing such release over the mortgage right object exceeding the purchase price.

307. If there are more than one mortgage right on a mortgage right object and there is no consensus among the holders of mortgage right about the release of mortgage right object from imposition exceeding the purchase price, the purchaser of the object may file an application to the Chairman of District Court to stipulate the release and simultaneously determine the sharing of auction proceeds among the creditors and

399. Consolidation means a legal act conducted by two companies or more to consolidate themselves by forming one new company which by law will receive assets and liabilities from the consolidating companies and consequently, the status of legal entity that consolidates is terminated (Art. 1 point 10 of Company Law).
400. *Ibid.*, p. 131.
401. Article 18 para. (1) of Mortgage Law.
402. Elucidation of Art. 18 para. (1) of Mortgage Law.
403. Article 18 para. (1) second sub paragraph of Mortgage Law.
404. Article 18 para. (4) of Mortgage Law.
405. Elucidation of Art. 18 para. (1), third sub paragraph of Mortgage Law.
406. Article 19 para. (1) of Mortgage Law and its elucidation.

their ranking in accordance with the prevailing laws and regulations. Holders of mortgage right who have not reached agreement shall use their best endeavour to reach agreement over the release of mortgage right object before the application is filed by the purchaser to the Chairman of District Court. When needed, the parties may appoint a mediator. Considering the distribution of sales proceed of the mortgage right object, the Chairman of District Court will have to consider the rankings among the holders of mortgage right.[407]

308. The application to release imposition of mortgage right cannot be filed by the purchaser of the object if such a purchase is conducted in a voluntary transaction while the parties have expressly stipulated in the deed of granting a mortgage right that the object shall not be released from the mortgage right.[408]

309. If the grantor of mortgage right is declared bankrupt, the holder of mortgage right shall remain vested with the authority to exercise all its rights.[409] Similar provision is also regulated under Law Number 37 of 2004 on Bankruptcy and Postponement of Obligation of Debt Payment ('Bankruptcy Law'). This right however is postponed at the latest ninety days since the bankruptcy decision is announced,[410] unless the receiver or supervisory judge decides cancellation of postponement after considering the time frame of postponement that is already underway, protection of the creditor and third party, possibility of settlement, consequence of postponement to the ongoing business concern and management of the debtor as well as the administration of bankrupt asset.[411] This period will be null and void by virtue of law when the bankruptcy is terminated or on the commencement of insolvency. Furthermore, the receiver is entitled to use the bankrupt assets in the form of movable property or immovable property or to sell the bankrupt asset for the interest of the ongoing business concern of the debtor, to the extent that a feasible protection has already been given to the separatist creditor or third party.[412] If the separatist creditor is able to prove that some of his receivables will be unable to be paid-off from the sale of secured property, may request entitlements of concurrent creditors for part of the receivables, without diminishing his right as separatist creditor.[413]

407. Article 19 para. (3) of Mortgage Law and its elucidation.
408. Article 19 para. (4) of Mortgage Law.
409. Article 21 of Mortgage Law.
410. Article 56 para. (1) of Bankruptcy Law.
411. Article 57 paras (2), (3), (4), (5) and (6) of Mortgage Law.
412. Article 56 para. (3) of Bankruptcy Law.
413. Article 138 of Bankruptcy Law.

Chapter 2. Securities in Movable Property (see also Parts II and IV)

§1. Privileges, Liens, Charges

310. The priority of debts in respect of certain specific assets is as follows:

(1) Court charges which specifically result from the disposal of a movable or immovable asset. These shall be paid from the proceeds of the sale of the assets over all other priority debts, and even over a pledge or mortgage.
(2) Unpaid consideration for the sale of movable assets.
(3) The costs incurred in the maintenance of the property.
(4) The wages owing to employees for the work carried out to the property.
(5) Anything delivered to a traveller by an innkeeper.
(6) Freight costs and additional charges.
(7) The compensation and payment for which public officials are responsible, due to negligence, error, violations, and misdemeanour, which were committed during the course of their service.[414]

311. The priority loans in regard to the movable and immovable properties in general are as follows and are claimed in the following order:

(1) The legal charges exclusively caused by sale of property as a result of execution of court decision over claim on ownership or control and saving of the estate; is prioritized over pledges and mortgages.
(2) The funeral charges, if they are excessive, without prejudice to the authority of the judges.
(3) All costs incurred in relation to the last illness.
(4) Employee's wages during the last year and that which is due for the current year, including the amount of any raise of such wage pursuant to Article 1602q of ICC; the amount of expenses incurred by an employee for the employer; the amount owned by the employer to an employee; the amount owed by the employer to an employee at the termination of his service; the amount due by the employer to an employee's family upon the employee's death.
(5) The debt claim against delivery of food to the debtor and his family, during the last six months.
(6) The debt claims of boarding schools for the most recent year.
(7) The debt claims of minors or individuals under conservatorship filed against their guardians and conservators, in respect of their management, to the extent that this cannot be compensated for by the mortgages or other security, which were put up pursuant to the fifteenth chapter of the first book of ICC, including the

414. Article 1139 of ICC.

payments due by the parents pursuant to the first book for the support and education of their minor legally acknowledged children.[415]

§2. Pledge

312. Provisions on pledge under ICC already existed for more than 100 years. New necessities emerge in a progressing society which at the beginning has not been thought of by the lawmakers. In fact, there are general provisions that at the beginning intended to be applicable for all types of pledge, but facing difficulties on its implementation, since at the time lawmakers prepared the provisions on pledge, they only remember that pledge is for tangible movable property.[416]

313. A pledge is a right which is obtained by a creditor in a movable property, which has been provided to him by the debtor or his representative, to secure a debt, and which entitles the creditor's priority over the other creditors with regard to the settlement of the debt, with the exception of the costs incurred in the sale of the asset to execute decision over ownership or possession, and the costs incurred to maintain it, after the pledge, and which must be prioritized.[417] The term 'pledge' refers to pledge right and also the pledged property.

314. Aside to pledge instance (pawn), a pledge over movable property in Anglo-Saxon legal system also knows other form called as 'chattel mortgage'. Different than a pledge, in chattel mortgage, other than possession, an ownership over movable property is also transferred from the pledger to the pledgee. Its legal consequence is very clear in execution of pledge, namely when the secured loan with a pledge is not repaid when it is due. In pawn that is similar to a pledge according to Indonesian law, if the loan is not repaid, then its execution must be through a public sale. Whereas, in chattel mortgage, if the loan is not repaid then the holder of chattel mortgage can immediately 'own' the property since the ownership of that property, when the security agreement was made, was directly transferred to the pledgee.[418]

315. A pledge is regarded as a limited property right. The following are the legal principles of pledge:[419]

(1) Provisions on pledge are compulsory. From the provisions set forth in the ICC on pledge, it is understood that those cannot be waived.
(2) A pledge may be transferred. Since a pledge is born as a result of its principal agreement, it means that a pledge may be transferred through a transfer of secured receivable.
(3) A pledge is individual, which means that a pledged property is attached to its receivable wholly. If the debtor dies and then the loan is inherited to his heirs, the pledge right over the pledged property is not dividable.

415. Article 1149 of ICC.
416. J. Satrio, S.H., *Hukum Jaminan Hak Jaminan Kebendaan*, p. 95 (Citra Aditya Bakti 1996).
417. Article 1150 of ICC.
418. Munir Fuady, *Hukum Jaminan Utang*, p. 153 (Erlangga 2013).
419. Kartini Muljadi – Gunawan Widjaja, *Hak Istimewa, Gadai, dan Hipotek*, pp. 182–196 (Kencana 2005).

(4) A pledge is total, which means that the pledged property includes all of its attachments, which is integral with the pledged property.
(5) A pledge cannot be divided. An owner of property is unable to release part of its ownership. It means that a pledge includes the whole of the pledge property and not only partly.
(6) A pledge follows its property (*droit de suite*). This is the fundamental character of property right. To whoever the pledged property is transferred, the pledge is still operative and executable.
(7) A pledge is prioritized (*droit de preference*). Article 1133 of ICC stipulates that the prioritized rights among the creditors emerges from the privileges, from pledge and hypothec.
(8) A pledge as limited (*jura in re aliena*). This principle is the continuance of *droit de preference*, where the pledge is only for the repayment of loan. A pledge is thus only an accessory.

316. A pledge agreement is proved by the same means as those used to prove its principal agreement.[420] Since a principal agreement can be any type of obligation agreement, but normally a loan agreement, and in principle, obligation agreement does not have specific form, can be made verbally, in writing, with authentic deed or privately drawn deed, then a pledge agreement is not bound to any specific form.[421]

317. A pledge is agreed with a purpose to provide security over specific obligation, which in general, not always a loan agreement. The pledge agreement is an accessory to its principal agreement. Essentially, a pledge can be used to secure a certain obligation. As an accessory agreement, pledge agreement has the following characteristics:

(1) is unable to be independent;
(2) its existence or removal depends on its principal agreement;
(3) if the principal agreement is transferred, the accessory agreement will also be transferred.

318. Further, if the pledge agreement is nullified since it violates provisions on pledge that is obligatory, but its principal agreement is applicable to the extent the principal agreement is made validly according to ICC. The right of pledge itself cannot be transferred without the transfer of its principal agreement, but in vice versa, the transfer of a principal agreement will concurrently transfer the pledge.[422]

319. Giving pledge is included as ownership act (*beschikking*), and *beschikking* is a legal action that carries or has huge consequence. It is normal therefore to pledge, an authority is required, a special authority, not just capacity of the person. But there is an exception to this provision which states that an authority of pledger cannot be brought forward to the pledgee. This is similar to Article 1977 paragraph (1) of ICC which states that the possession of movable properties constitutes absolute ownership. This means that third party can assume that the person holding a movable property is the owner of it, and therefore that person is authorized to do actions over the property.

420. Article 1151 of ICC.
421. J. Satrio, S.H., *Hukum Jaminan Hak Jaminan Kebendaan*, p. 110 (Citra Aditya Bakti 1996).
422. *Ibid.*, pp. 110–111.

A protection must be given to all parties obtaining a movable property, including the pledgee.[423]

320. Pledge involves two parties, the pledger as debtor and pledgee as creditor. It is also possible that based on consent by the parties, the pledged property is held by third party. The delivery of possession over pledged property to the creditor (or designated third party) is a forceful law, and therefore it cannot be deviated by the parties. If this is deviated, it would mean that the agreement will become fiducia that is subject to fiduciary security law.[424]

321. A pledge right in respect of tangible movable property and debts payable to bearer shall be established by placing the pledge in the power of the creditor or a third party, who has been mutually agreed upon by the parties. It is not applicable to assets, which are left in the power of the debtor or the pledger, or which shall be returned if the creditor so desires. It becomes void if the pledge is no longer controlled by the pledgee. If this occurs as a result of loss or transfer, the pledger has the right to reclaim it under Article 1977 paragraph (2) of ICC[425] and upon the return of the pledged property, the pledge right shall be considered to have never been lost. The absence of authority of the pledgee to dispose of the property cannot be denied by the creditor who has taken such properties in pledge, without prejudice to the right to reclaim by the individual who has lost the asset or from whom it was taken.[426]

322. Scholten says that a pledge can be made over an invoice, hence a pledge of tangible property. The right to collect that is realized by the invoice is also obtained by the pledgee, since the pledger has the invoice in his possession, the pledgee will be considered as the rightful party. Pitlo has another opinion. What is pledged is the right to collect, but since the owner of invoice to the order and of bearer paper, which is unable to show the invoice, cannot validate that he is a creditor, hence, the invoice is also delivered even though the right to collect the invoice was already pledged.[427]

323. A pledge over registered receivables is made by notification to the debtor. , With regards to pledge of receivables, there are no requirements to perform a cessie. If there is a cessie, then by making the deed of cessie, the delivery is made. For pledge, it is deemed implemented when it is notified to the debtor, without the necessity of making a cessie. Notification by the creditor to the debtor that the receivables are pledged to the third party is considered as the same as releasing secured property from the debtor's possession. HR gave considerations as follows:

423. *Ibid.*, p. 112.

424. Munir Fuady, *Hukum Jaminan Utang*, p. 155 (Erlangga 2013).

425. Article 1977 of ICC regulates that an individual who loses something, may, during a period of three years effective as of the date that the loss or theft took place, claim the lost or stolen item as his property from the individual with whom he finds the items, without prejudice to the right of the latter mentioned to demand indemnification from the individual who delivered the items to him, also without prejudice to provisions under Art. 582 of ICC. Article 582 of ICC stipulates that a person, who claims the return of transferred or lost properties, is not required to return the sale price paid to the current holder of the properties, unless the holder has purchased the properties at an annual or other market, public auction, or from a seller who is known to usually trade in such objects.

426. Article 1152 of ICC.

427. J. Satrio, S.H., *Hukum Jaminan Hak Jaminan Kebendaan*, p. 116 (Citra Aditya Bakti 1996).

(1) According to Article 1150 of ICC a pledged property must be released from the pledgor's possession and deliver to the pledgee's possession.
(2) As movable tangible properties, a pledge is granted by way of releasing from his powers to the pledgee personally or to the third party, agreed by the parties, also by granting a pledge over receivables are made by notification to the debtor.
(3) Through that notification, the relationship between the debtor and creditor is temporarily terminated, with a consequence that the latter, even though maintaining his ownership over pledged receivable and authorized to take *beschikking* action over pledged receivables, has released his rights arising out of the receivables against the debtor.[428]

324. A pledge is a property right over movable property owned by other party. This is not specifically stated in the ICC. But since there is a right of pledgee, in case the pledged property is lost or stolen, the pledgee is entitled to reclaim it from the third party. This provision means that the pledgee holds *droit de suite* principle over pledged property, namely pledge right follows the property with whomever the properties are held. Reclaim right under ICC is similar to the *revindicatoir* right of an owner.[429]

325. Even though a pledge right is a property right, but this property right is different than the property right such as right of ownership that gives enjoyment to the owner. In this matter, the property right, namely pledge, is a security property right. This right is related to the personal right.[430]

326. In addition to the endorsement, the delivery of the paper is also required to establish the pledge right on bearer paper.[431]

327. Pledge right to intangible movable properties, with the exception of those evidenced on bearer paper, shall be established by notification of the pledge to the individual, against whom the pledged right shall be exercised. He may claim written proof of the notification and the consent of the pledgees.[432]

328. If the debtor or pledger is unable to comply with his obligations, the creditor is not allowed to transfer the pledged property to become his ownership. Any stipulations otherwise regulated shall be null and void.[433] Supreme Court has provided considerations on this matter, namely, the legal principle of loan agreement of money with a security prohibit, that in case of default of the debtor, the secured property will automatically become the ownership of the creditor. Therefore, a provision in the loan agreement which stipulates the same is nullified and does not have any legal power.[434]

329. The above provision is to protect the debtor, which is normally in a weaker position, and accordingly, heavy terms must be accepted. Furthermore, if there is no prohibition on the legal principle as mentioned above, a creditor may expect that the debtor is in default so that the creditor can take ownership over the pledged property.

428. *Ibid.*, pp. 118–119.
429. Article 226 of Updated Indonesian Regulation (HIR).
430. *Ibid.*, p. 109 (Citra Aditya Bakti 1996).
431. Article 1152 *bis* of ICC.
432. Article 1153 of ICC.
433. Article 1154 of ICC.
434. J. Satrio, S.H., *Hukum Jaminan Hak Jaminan Kebendaan*, pp. 126–127 (Citra Aditya Bakti 1996).

If this happens, the banking system may be disturbed since creditor has other interests than just a repayment of loan.

330. Article 1154 of ICC stipulates prohibition prior to the formation of pledge, before the debtor is in default, when the debtor defaults, the pledged property will be owned by the creditor. Forming an agreement, after the debtor defaults, that the creditor will transfer the pledged property by considering the repayment of debtor's debt, is not prohibited.[435]

331. Unless the parties otherwise stipulate, in the event that the debtor or the pledger does not comply with his obligations, the creditor shall be authorized, following the lapse of a specific term or in the event that no specific term was stipulated, after a summons in respect of compliance, to sell the pledge in public pursuant to local customs and in accordance with the usual requirements, to settle the debt which includes the interest and costs incurred from the proceeds of the sale. If the pledge is of commercial items sold at the market or securities traded on the stock market, then the sale can also take place in such locations, provided that two agents are involved in such business as intermediaries.[436]

332. The provision of Article 1155 of ICC is complementary, since the parties are free to regulate otherwise. To the extent the parties do not deviate from that provision, then Article 1155 of ICC is operative.[437] If the debtor or pledger defaults, then the pledgee is authorized to sell the pledged property in public according to customs and traditions locally. This right is obtained by the creditor if the debtor or pledger is in default. This right is only born at the time debtor defaults. This is provided under the law, not necessarily be regulated through an agreement.[438] Previously this provision emerged only when the parties agree to it, but at the moment, this is applicable by virtue of law.[439] Execution title is not required to conduct the sale. A pledgee can execute without interference of court, bailiff, or prior seizure. This right is called as *parate executie*. Only the pledgee has this type of right. A hypothec holder also has the same right provided that it is agreed by the parties. Hence, the right exists if there is an agreement between the parties.[440]

333. If the debtor or the pledger fails to fulfil his obligations, the creditor may demand in court that the pledge shall be sold to satisfy the debt including the interest and costs, in the manner to be determined by the judge, or the judge admits the creditor's request that the pledge shall be retained by him, until an amount has been determined in the judgment to pay off the debt and the interest and costs.[441] The background of this provision is due to certain properties will not profitable if they are sold in public sale, such as registered receivables. The pledgee may also request the judge to determine that the pledgee will purchase the pledged property with the price determined by the judge. This authority is useful for a pledged property which its price has been reduced significantly. A public sale may be a loss to both parties, creditor and debtor. Worry

435. *Ibid.*, p. 129.
436. Article 1155 of ICC.
437. *Ibid.*, p. 134.
438. *Ibid.*, p. 134.
439. *Ibid.*, p. 135.
440. J. Satrio, S.H., *Hukum Jaminan Hak Jaminan Kebendaan*, p. 135 (Citra Aditya Bakti 1996).
441. Article 1156 para. (1) of ICC.

on the cheat by the creditor can be exempted since the judge will determine the price with his decision, whether or not it is permitted and its purchase price.[442]

334. With regard to the transfer of the pledge mentioned herein and in Article 1155 of ICC, the creditor is required to notify the pledger by not later than the following day if there is a daily postal service or telegram communication, or else by the first departing mail. Notification by telegram or registered letter shall be regarded as proper notification.[443]

335. The creditor is responsible for the loss or depreciation of the pledged property, to the extent that this is caused by his negligence. On the other hand, the debtor is obligated to remedy the creditor all expenses that are useful and have to be spent by the creditor to save the pledged property.[444] Expenses that are useful and necessary will differ case by case.

336. If a loan is pledged, and interest accrues on this loan, the creditor may set off the interest against the amount which is due to him. If no interest accrues on the debt secured by the pledged loan, then the interest received by the pledgee shall be deducted from the principal sum.[445] This means that a creditor or pledgee has a preferential right to be repaid, since it entitles the pledgee to compensate his interest before other creditors.[446]

337. To the extent the pledgee does not misuse the pledged property, the debtor is not authorized to reclaim the pledged property before he pays in full, for the principal, interest, and loan's expenses that is secured with the pledge, together with all incurred expenses to save the pledge.[447] If a second loan arises between the same debtor and same creditor, following the pledge, and collectible prior to the payment, or on the date of the payment of the first debt, then the creditor is not obligated to dispose the pledged property, prior to full settlement of both of his debts, even though no stipulations have been made to secure the pledge for payment of the second debt.[448]

338. A pledge cannot be divided, notwithstanding that the debt among the heirs of the debtor or of the creditor can be divided. The heir of the debtor, who has paid his share of the debt, cannot claim the return of his share in the pledge until the debt has been fully settled. At the same time the heir of a creditor who has received his share in the debt cannot return the pledge thereby jeopardizing the co-heirs who have not been paid yet.[449] Most of the time a debtor has a wrong understanding about pledge. He thinks that if he repays half of the debt, half of the pledged property will also be released. Thus, if he owes Rp 1 million, and gives security for that debt, and after repays the first loan he owes another Rp 2 million and as a security gives additional property; if he repays part of his debt, for example the Rp 1 million then normally he would think that he is entitled to get back one of the pledged properties. Based on the legal principle when a pledge is not able to be divided, the pledgee is entitled to hold

442. *Ibid.*, p. 142.
443. Article 1156 para. (2) of ICC.
444. Article 1157 of ICC.
445. Article 1158 of ICC.
446. *Ibid.*, p. 143.
447. Article 1159 para. (1) of ICC.
448. Article 1159 para. (2) of ICC.
449. Article 1160 of ICC.

all pledged properties until his receivable is fully repaid. Each loan (and part of it) adds each part and all pledged properties as unitary, not as a stand-alone property, even though the properties are divided. Further, if the receivable itself is able to be divided, it does not mean that it will cause the pledged property to be divided in accordance with the value of receivables.[450]

339. Right of pledge is removed due to:[451]

(1) Expiry of principal agreement that is secured with pledge; this is in conforming to the accessory character of the pledge so that its applicability depends on its principal agreement. A principal agreement is terminated, among others, as a result of, repayment, compensation, novation, and debt release.
(2) Detachment of pledged property from the pledgee's possession; despite this fact, the pledgee is still entitled to reclaim the pledged property and if he is successful, law considers that the pledge agreement is not terminated.
(3) Removal or annihilation of the pledged property.
(4) Voluntary release of the pledged property.
(5) By way of mixture, where the pledgee become the owner of the pledged property.

340. All provisions on pledge are not applicable to tradable properties, to the extent the Indonesian Commercial Code already give their stipulations; it is also not applicable to state-owned banks giving the loan provided that they have a deviated provisions agreed between the bank and the debtor; a pledge instance also has its own regulation.[452]

§3. Retention Right, Compensation

341. There is no one chapter dedicated for retention right, but they are scattered in several chapters within ICC and even in other law.

342. Employees holding something owned by other person in order to perform his work on that property is entitled to retain that property until his remuneration and related expenses are repaid, except if the remuneration and expenses of employee has been guaranteed by the employer.[453] This provision is regulated under service agreement in ICC.

343. On a different chapter of deposit, ICC stipulates that the receiver of deposit is entitled to retain the deposited property as long as all losses have not been fully repaid due to its deposit.[454]

450. J. Satrio, S.H., *Hukum Jaminan Hak Jaminan Kebendaan*, pp. 145–146 (Citra Aditya Bakti 1996).
451. *Ibid.*, pp. 146–147.
452. *Ibid.*, p. 148.
453. Article 1616 of ICC.
454. Article 1729 of ICC.

344. In another chapter of granting proxy authorization, ICC stipulates that the authorized is entitled to retain the property of authorizer possessed by the authorized until all his demands as a result of proxy have been fully repaid.[455]

345. When a debtor is declared bankrupt by a court decision, the retention right is not lost.[456] As per provisions under ICC, Bankruptcy Law explains that this retention right will be valid until the debt is fully repaid.

§4. Delegation, Direct Claim (Possibly Created by Statute Law to Claim Payment Directly from the Debtor of One's Debt)

346. ICC stipulates that each payment presumes a debt; each payment that is not made pursuant to a debt may be reclaimed.[457] With regard to the unrestricted obligation (*natuurljike verbintenis*), which was fulfilled voluntarily, it cannot be reclaimed.[458] It can be concluded that the unrestricted obligation is an obligation where the creditor is not entitled to reclaim the implementation of performance even with judge's assistance. In contrast, the debtor does not have the legal obligation to do the performance. Debtor only has moral obligations to fulfil it, such as, payment of interest that was not agreed before[459] and debt payment as a result of gambling.[460]

347. An individual who has consciously or unconsciously received something which is not compulsory to be paid to him shall return it to the person giving the thing.[461] Meaning of payment is every fulfilment of performance, whether it is a debt payment that is not compulsory or delivery of something that is not compulsory.[462]

348. If an individual, due to his fault thinks that he has debt, pays his debt, then he is entitled to reclaim what has been paid to the creditor. Nevertheless, the right will be lost if, as a result of that payment, the creditor has destroyed letter of indebtedness without diminishing that person's right who has paid it to reclaim from the actual debtor.

455. Article 1812 of ICC.
456. Article 61 of Bankruptcy Law.
457. Article 1359 para. (1) of ICC.
458. Article 1359 para. (2) of ICC.
459. Article 1766 of ICC.
460. Prof. Dr Mariam Darus Badrulzaman, *Hukum Perikatan dalam KUH Perdata Buku Ketiga*, pp. 139–140 (1st edition. Citra Aditya Bakti 2015).
461. Article 1360 of ICC.
462. *Ibid.*, p. 143.

Selected Bibliography

Amiruddin Pabbu, S. M. (2014). *Pengantar Ilmu Hukum.* Mitra Wacana Media.

Apeldoorn, P. M. (1996). *Pengantar Ilmu Hukum.* Pradnya Paramita.

Badrulzaman, M. D. (2000). *Beberapa Permasalahan Hukum Hak Jaminan.* Yayasan Pengembangan Hukum Bisnis.

Badrulzaman, M. D. (2015). *Hukum Perikatan dalam KUH Perdata Buku Ketiga.* Citra Aditya Bakti.

Collins Dictionary. (2017). Retrieved from Collins Dictionary: https://www.collinsdictionary.com/dictionary/english/insolvent.

Fuady, M. (2013). *Hukum Jaminan Utang.* Erlangga.

Hadisoeprapto, H. (1984). *Seri Hukum Perdata: Pokok-Pokok Hukum Perdata dan Hukum Jaminan.* Indhill Co.

Harsono, P.B. (2008). *Hukum Agraria Indonesia: Sejarah Pembentukan Undang-Undang Pokok Agraria, Isi dan Pelaksanaannya.* Djambatan.

J. B. Daliyo, S. (1997). *Pengantar Hukum Indonesia.* Gramedia Pustaka Utama.

Limbong, B. (2012). *Konflik Pertanahan.* Margaretha Pustaka.

Mokhammad Najih, S.M. (2014). *Pengantar Hukum Indonesia: Sejarah, Konsep Tata Hukum, dan Politik Hukum Indonesia.* Malang: Setara Press.

Muljadi, K., & Widjaja, G. (2005). *Seri Hukum Harta Kekayaan: Hak Istimewa, Gadai, dan Hipotek.* Jakarta: Prenada Media Group.

National Geographic. (n.d.). Retrieved from Nat Geo Sites: http://travel.nationalgeographic.com/travel/countries/indonesia-facts/.

Prof. Arie S. Hutagalung, S.M. (2015). *The Principles of Indonesian Agrarian Law.* Badan Penerbit FHUI.

Prof. Dr Jimly Asshiddiqie, S. (2009). *The Constitutional Law of Indonesia.* Sweet & Maxwell Asia.

Prof. Dr Peter Mahmud Marzuki, S.M. (2013). *Pengantar Ilmu Hukum.* Prenadamedia Group.

Prof. Dr St. Remy Sjahdeni, S. (1999). *Hak Tanggungan: Asas-Asas, Ketentuan-Ketentuan Pokok dan Masalah Yang Dihadapi Oleh Perbankan.* Alumni.

Rachmadi Usman, S.M. (2011). *Hukum Kebendaan.* Sinar Grafika.

Satrio, J. (1996). *Hukum Jaminan Hak Jaminan Kebendaan.* Bandung: Citra Aditya Bakti.

Sedyawati, E. (2008). *KeIndonesiaan dalam Budaya.*

Subekti, P. (1979). *Pokok-Pokok Hukum Perdata.* Intermasa.

Suparman, M. (2015). *Hukum Waris Perdata.* Sinar Grafika.

Treaty. (n.d.). Retrieved from Wikipedia: https://en.wikipedia.org/wiki/Treaty.

Usman, R. (2008). *Hukum Jaminan Keperdataan.* Jakarta: Sinar Grafika.

Widjaja, K. M. (2003). *Kebendaan pada Umumnya.* Kencana.

Widjaja, K. M. (2004). *Kedudukan Berkuasa dan Hak Milik.* Kencana.

Widjaja, K. M. (2005). *Hak Istimewa, Gadai, dan Hipotek.* Kencana.

World Culture Encyclopedia. (n.d.). Retrieved from Culture of Indonesia: http://www.everyculture.com/Ge-It/Indonesia.html.

Table of Cases

The numbers here refer to paragraph numbers.

Decision Number 210/K/Sip/1955, 107
Decision Number 239/K/Sip/1957, 107
HgH. Dated 18 August 1932, 233
Hoog Gerechts Hof (HGH) dated 25 October 1934, 197
Supreme Court decision Number 187 K/SIP/1956 dated 10 January 1957, 100
Supreme Court decisions Number 394 K/Pdt/1984 dated 31 May 1985, 285
Supreme Court decision Number 329 K/SIP/1957 dated 24 September 1958, 196

Index

The numbers here refer to paragraph numbers.

1945 Constitution, 7

Abandonment, 212, 288, 304
Absolute, 15, 16, 44, 49, 87, 94, 139, 175–178, 192, 230, 287, 319
Accession, 198–201, 280
Accessory agreement, 242, 281, 317
Acquisitieve verjaring, 196
Administrator, 217
Adult, 197
Agrarian law, 32, 47–50, 59, 60, 64, 65, 91, 95–97, 100, 101, 103–105, 107–109, 112, 114–116, 131–133, 136–139, 167, 168, 170, 190, 194–196, 198, 201, 209, 275
Agreement, 42, 43, 46, 51, 54, 64, 68, 75, 86, 101, 106, 109, 110, 112, 154, 168, 173, 174, 176, 177, 182, 199, 202, 219, 220, 223, 224, 226, 230, 233, 236, 238, 242, 244, 246–248, 250, 253, 260, 261, 264–266, 274, 280–283, 288, 293, 307, 314–318, 320, 328, 330, 332, 339, 342
Agriculture, 103, 231
Aircraft, 122, 123, 240
Algemene Verordening, 16
Anglo-saxon, 314
Animal husbandry, 62, 103
Annulment, 288, 304
Appropriation, 89, 202–205
Arbitrary, 194
Asian, 37
Assets, 16, 18, 44, 86, 144, 158, 161, 183, 186, 202–205, 216, 217, 221, 273, 274, 276, 303, 309, 310, 313, 321
Auction, 98, 264, 272, 276, 288, 290, 291, 300, 305, 307
Authorized, 74, 88, 98, 104, 168, 174, 186, 202, 226–228, 236, 257, 272, 319, 323, 331, 332, 337, 344
Authors, 232

Bad faith, 85, 146, 152, 153, 203
Banker's clause, 288
Bank guarantee, 246, 282
Bankruptcy, 216, 217, 236, 263, 309, 345
Beschikking, 319, 323
Besluiten Regerings, 15–17
Bhinneka Tunggal Ika, 4
Board of directors, 295
Bond, 154, 249, 254
Bondholders, 249
Book of land, 93, 117, 126, 287, 294, 298, 301
BOT. *See* Build, operate, and transfer (BOT)
BTO. *See* Build, transfer, and operate (BTO)
Building, 57, 63, 65, 90, 98, 103, 104, 106, 113, 118, 126–127, 133–135, 140, 164, 168, 170, 171, 183, 198, 201, 208, 215, 239, 240, 279
Build, operate, and transfer (BOT), 106
Build, transfer, and operate (BTO), 106
Burgerlijk Wetboek, 22
Business day, 301
Business entity, 158, 205

Cabinet, 8, 10
Capital alliance, 202
Cash, 58, 136, 164, 166, 256
Central, 7, 16, 214
Certificate, 92–95, 98, 110, 117, 125, 126, 139, 140, 154, 187, 254, 256, 257, 262, 283, 286, 288, 292, 297, 301
Cessie, 259, 323

Index

Charges, 105–106, 269–274, 277, 278, 310–311
Chattel mortgage, 314
Chinese, 22, 71, 188
Chinese foreign east, 22
Citizen, 3, 188
Civil law, 17, 22, 73, 122, 187
Claim, 58, 68, 90, 93, 94, 99, 139, 140, 146, 151, 154, 179, 197, 219, 251, 262, 292, 311, 327, 338, 346–348
Claimant, 146, 197
Class action, 135
Clause, 32, 38, 49, 115, 288
Closed law, 45
Codification, 17
Colonization, 15, 26
Communities, 138, 141, 190, 195, 214
Compliance, 76, 274, 293, 331
Compulsory, 174, 187, 315
Concordance, 22, 73
Concurrent creditors, 309
Condominium, 124, 126, 127, 173
Condominium unit, 125–127, 172, 173, 187
Conflict, 18, 75, 138, 139, 142
Constitutional Court, 10
Constitution of Republic of Indonesia Union, 27
Consumable, 55, 143
Costs, 74, 183, 186, 228, 246, 274, 310, 311, 313, 331, 333
Covenant, 43, 112–113, 265, 266, 288, 289, 291, 293
Credietverband, 115, 275
Credit, 181, 275
Creditor, 39, 76, 116, 118, 181–183, 217–220, 230–271, 276, 282, 283, 285, 288, 291, 293, 301–303, 307, 309, 313, 315, 320–323, 328–338, 346, 348
Criminal, 22, 210, 268
Criminal law, 22
Cultivators, 211
Custom, 42, 43, 73, 331, 332
Customary law, 14, 21, 22, 43, 73, 97, 99, 100, 136, 137, 196, 198, 201, 256, 280

Daendels, 15
Damages, 74, 112, 132, 228
Death, 74, 78, 148, 186–188, 311
Debt, 54, 116–118, 183, 217, 219, 224, 244, 246–248, 250, 261, 262, 264, 266–268, 271, 274, 276, 282, 283, 285, 288, 289, 293, 297, 304, 305, 309, 311, 313, 330, 331, 333, 336–339, 345–348
Debtor, 39, 118, 181–183, 217–220, 230, 232, 234, 236–238, 246, 248, 257, 264–269, 274, 276, 282, 283, 288–293, 297, 300, 309, 311, 313, 315, 320, 321, 323, 328–333, 335, 337, 338, 340, 345–348
Decision, 10, 16, 43, 48, 64, 99, 100, 142, 197, 217, 220, 233, 257, 276, 285, 288, 292, 309, 311, 313, 333, 345
Deed, 76, 77, 79, 81, 98, 110, 162, 187, 188, 201, 243–245, 249, 253, 256, 257, 259, 266, 283, 286, 288, 292, 293, 297–299, 301, 308, 316, 323
Defendant
 definition, 197
Delegation, 7, 288, 346–348
Delivery, 49, 51–53, 89, 230, 232, 234, 235, 238, 256, 260, 311, 320, 323, 326, 347
Den Haag, 27
Direct claim, 346–348
Dispute, 10, 43, 74, 80, 139, 140, 186, 195
District court, 288, 304, 305, 307
Doctrine, 42, 43
Domestic capital, 158
Domestic investment, 35
Domiciled, 62–65, 171, 220, 297
Dominus, 226, 229
Droit de preference, 315
Droit de suite, 284, 315, 324
Dutch, 11–15, 17, 26, 71, 288
Dutch East Indies, 17, 21–24, 27, 71–73
Dutch East Indies Government, 15–37

Earth, 48, 49
Easement, 108
Eigenaar, 238
Eigendom, 98, 232, 234
Emergency, 43
Environmental, 133, 159
Equitable, 95–100, 180

Index

Erfpacht, 49
Estate, 58, 59, 70–82, 219, 311
European, 11, 19, 22, 71, 73
Evidence, 92–94, 96–99, 126, 139, 140, 154, 187, 188, 195, 257, 261, 292, 301, 327
Execution, 51, 54, 110, 246, 248, 257, 264, 267, 282, 288, 292, 311, 314, 332
Exhausted, 55
Expropriation, 87, 206–215

Facility, 126, 127, 173, 214
Farm, 56, 62, 169, 170, 197, 231
Federal state
  fiducia, 184, 320
Fiducia cum amico, 222–268
  fiduciary security, 222, 232, 234, 235, 239–245, 247–268
Fiduciairus, 235, 236, 239
Fiduciary, 50, 78–82, 118, 121, 183, 184, 222, 232, 234, 235, 239–245, 247–268, 320
Fishery, 62, 103
Five Principles, 3, 4
Foreign capital, 158
Foreign east, 19, 22, 71, 73, 188
Foreigner, 64, 65, 158, 161, 171, 172
Foreign investment, 35, 159
Foreign legal entity, 64, 65, 158, 171
Form, 58, 69, 74, 90, 96, 99, 106, 110, 154, 158, 166, 186, 187, 195, 231, 233, 234, 263, 282, 288, 309, 314, 316
Formal law, 42
Foundation, 127, 201, 204
Fragmentation, 51–54, 70–77
Funds, 157–161, 248, 300
Furnishing, 162, 164–166
Furniture, 162, 165, 166

Gestor, 226–229
God, 3, 257, 292
Good faith, 85, 93, 97, 99, 146, 151–153, 194, 195, 197, 255
Goods, 49, 50, 57, 67, 68, 106, 116, 118–122, 128, 129, 161, 162, 165
Grantor, 226, 231, 235, 239, 249, 252, 253, 258, 259, 263, 264, 266, 267, 278, 283, 288–291, 294, 295, 297, 309
Grondwet, 18
Grosse deed, 292
Ground rent, 90
Gun seirei, 23

Heir, 74, 77, 78, 80, 81, 148, 186–188, 197, 227, 315, 338
Helicopter, 122, 123
Historical, 4, 41, 44–50
Horizontal, 136, 198, 201
House, 43, 56, 107, 162, 164–166, 172, 228
Household, 162, 164, 165, 228
Huurbeding, 288
Hypothec, 48, 49, 114, 115, 119, 120, 122, 123, 231, 240, 241, 260, 263, 275, 280, 284, 288, 292, 293, 300, 315, 332

Ideology, 4, 33
Immovable goods, 49, 50, 118–122
Imprisonment, 112, 268
Independence, 3, 11–38
Independence war, 27
Indigenous people, 11, 13, 14, 22
Indische Staatsregeling (IS), 20–22, 70–72
Individual, 78, 79, 83, 85, 87, 89, 93, 112, 124, 125, 128, 129, 145, 148–150, 156, 159, 174, 175, 177, 179, 185, 190–192, 194, 202, 204, 223–226, 229, 276, 293, 294, 296, 311, 315, 321, 327, 347, 348
Indonesian, 1–3, 6, 8, 10, 22, 32, 33, 61–66, 70, 71, 91, 100, 119, 120, 123, 140, 158, 171, 174, 188, 216, 243, 314, 340
Indonesian Civil Code (ICC), 32, 47–49, 51, 54, 56, 57, 82, 90, 100, 114, 115, 123, 128, 130, 131, 137, 153, 164, 167, 175, 176, 185, 192, 194, 202, 209, 219, 220, 222, 223, 225–227, 233, 247, 256, 259, 269, 275, 280, 284, 311, 312, 315, 318, 319, 323, 324, 330, 332, 334, 341–346
Indonesian Commercial Code, 120, 340
Indonesian Communist Party, 33
Indonesian law, 62–65, 216, 314
Infrastructure, 106, 133, 214
Inheritance, 49, 74, 80, 130, 186–188, 301
Inseparable, 43, 174, 293
Insolvency, 216–221, 309

Index

Insolvent, 216–220
Insurance, 251, 262, 288
Intangible, 55, 118, 154–156, 175, 180, 183, 184, 239, 241, 256, 327
Interest, 46, 49, 58, 59, 69, 74, 86, 87, 92–123, 132, 154, 159, 161, 174–184, 186, 192, 194, 203, 207, 209, 211, 214, 224–229, 246, 248, 249, 264, 276, 282, 288, 289, 305, 309, 329, 331, 333, 336, 337, 346
International, 43
International Court of Justice, 43
Investment, 35, 157–161, 205
Investor, 109, 158–161
Invoice, 140, 322

Japan, 23–24, 71
Joint equipment, 126, 127, 173
Joint-estate, 58, 59
Joint facility, 126, 127, 173
Joint land, 124, 126, 127, 173
Joint ownership, 124–130
Judex facti, 197
Judges, 10, 43, 74, 151, 152, 186, 220, 221, 228, 309, 311, 333, 346
Judicial, 43
Judicial Commission, 10
Judiciary, 10
Jurisprudence, 42, 43, 50

Koninklijk Besluit, 16, 19

Land, 98, 99, 132, 169, 206–209, 211–214
Land Conveyancing Officer *(Pejabat Pembuat Akta Tanah),* 98, 110, 283, 293, 297–299, 301
110
Land interest, 49, 58, 59, 110
Landlord, 104, 109, 111, 168, 201
Land registration, 92, 95, 97, 98, 142, 187, 188, 195
Land surface, 124
Lawful, 69
Lawmaker, 224, 312
Laws, 13, 14, 17, 18, 21, 22, 24, 26, 28–30, 32, 35, 36, 39–91, 93, 95–97, 99–101, 103–105, 107–109, 112–114, 122–124, 126, 131–133, 136, 137, 138i, 139, 141, 146, 154, 157–160, 162, 167, 168, 170, 172–176, 184, 186, 187, 190, 194–196, 198, 201, 202, 204–213, 216, 217, 221–224, 226, 238–241, 245, 247, 248, 250, 256, 259, 260, 263, 264, 268, 269, 271, 275, 276, 280, 288, 299, 301, 307, 309, 314, 320, 332, 339, 341, 345-348
Leasehold, 104
Led democracy, 33
Legal entity, 62–65, 132, 158, 171, 202–204, 294, 296, 297, 302
Legal relationship, 39, 40, 84, 86, 107, 112, 133, 177, 233, 283
Legal science, 45
Legal system, 314
Legatees, 76, 81
Letter, 34, 43, 98, 126, 140, 187, 188, 200, 211, 261, 262, 334, 348
Liabilities, 216, 303
Liable, 74
Licence, 109–111
Liens, 249–274, 300–311
Limited liability company, 160, 184, 202, 295
Loan agreement, 281–283, 293, 316, 317, 328
Lodging, 107
Logical, 86, 260

Mapping, 92
Market, 11, 58, 90, 214, 264, 331
Measurement letter, 126
Money, 12, 22, 39, 52, 68, 90, 129, 158, 182, 226, 242, 248, 300, 328
Money laundering, 210
Monopoly, 12
Mortgage, 275–309
Motto, 4
Movable goods, 49, 50, 67, 68, 118, 120

Nation, 2, 3, 6, 25, 211
National, 3, 4, 6, 158, 159, 188, 214, 215, 275
Nationality, 121, 123, 136
Natural resources, 48, 49
Natuurlijke verbintenis, 224
Negligence, 197, 228, 255, 310, 335
Negligent, 197

Index

Neighbouring land, 49, 132
Netherlands, 14, 18, 27, 73
New order, 34–37
Newspaper, 264
Notarial deed, 79, 81, 243, 293
Notary, 173, 188, 253
Novation, 219, 274, 339
Null, 265, 288, 289, 297, 299, 309, 328

Objective law, 40
Obligation, 40, 43, 49, 64, 86, 92, 98, 131, 132, 138, 176, 182, 200, 217–219, 227–230, 234, 242, 246, 252, 259, 269, 282, 309, 316, 317, 328, 331, 333, 346
Octrooi, 12
Official, 4, 64, 96, 98, 99, 187, 256, 310
Onverschuldigde betaling, 224
Opinion
  opstal right, 49
Osamu seirei, 23–24
Owner, 57, 69, 84, 85, 107, 109, 132, 145, 146, 151, 152, 170, 173, 174, 177, 187, 195, 197, 198, 200, 230, 235–239, 265, 279, 288, 297, 302, 304, 315, 319, 322, 325, 339
Ownership, 49, 51–69, 87–89, 98, 109, 111, 117, 124–130, 139, 140, 142, 172–174, 187, 189, 190, 192–196, 200, 201, 209, 212, 230, 232, 234–236, 238, 239, 244, 258, 260, 286, 297, 311, 313–315, 319, 323, 325, 328, 329

Pancasila, 4, 6, 34, 36
Parate executie, 332
Parliament, 8, 10, 18, 19
Partial deletion, 277
Part-ownership, 174
Patrimony, 70–82
Pawn, 314
Payable, 69, 161, 192, 266, 320
People, 2, 3, 8, 11, 13, 14, 19, 21, 22, 39, 64, 73, 95, 99, 124, 132, 138, 141, 142, 211, 240
People's Consultative Assembly, 9, 10, 38
People's Representative Council, 9
Period, 62–64, 75, 81, 95, 97, 99, 100, 103, 106, 109–111, 115, 194, 230–232, 267, 288, 304, 309
Permanent legal power, 292
Personal property, 67–69, 143–184
Personal right, 134, 173, 175–177, 179, 236, 238, 325
Philosophy, 6
Pitlo, 129, 238, 322
Plantation, 90, 103, 142, 144
Positive law, 24
Possess, 85, 88, 236, 283
Possession, 74, 83–89, 93, 97, 99, 141, 143–153, 180, 186, 189–197, 211, 231, 232, 236, 313, 314, 319, 320, 322, 323, 339
Power of attorney, 249
PPAT. *See* Land Conveyancing Officer *(Pejabat Pembuat Akta Tanah)*
Preferential, 116, 118, 183, 263, 276, 336
President Soeharto, 37
President Soekarno, 33
Principal agreement, 236, 242, 244, 246, 253, 260, 265, 266, 293, 315–318, 339
Principal loan, 246, 282
Principle, 3, 4, 22, 32, 43, 47, 73, 100, 136, 137, 141, 159, 169, 174, 198, 201, 203, 245, 252, 255, 261, 276–280, 282–290, 315, 316, 324, 328, 329, 338
Privately drawn deed, 259, 293, 316
Privilege, 74, 90, 269–274, 310–311, 315
Problem, 3, 51, 52, 131–142
Procedural law, 22
Promise, 98, 219, 230, 234, 291
Promulgated, 22, 35, 43, 50, 72, 114, 138, 201, 209
Promulgation, 17, 47, 49, 59, 95–97, 114, 131, 209, 275
Property law, 47, 174, 175
Provision, 26, 28, 112, 124, 132, 133, 136, 139, 147, 169, 173, 178, 187, 190, 192, 195, 200, 202, 209, 219, 227, 237, 239, 240, 246, 248–251, 255, 256, 258, 259, 261, 265–268, 276, 289, 293, 298, 299, 309, 319, 324, 328, 329, 332, 333, 342
Proxy, 183, 226, 227, 253, 344
Public, 207, 214

Publication system, 139
Publicity, 172, 174, 255, 287
Purchase price, 306-307, 333

Quorum, 295

Rank, 42, 298, 300
Ranking, 298, 304, 307
Real property, 55-66, 90-142
Receivables, 49, 74, 217, 219, 256, 259, 276, 288, 291, 296, 301-304, 309, 323, 333, 338
Rechtsverwerking, 196, 197
Recording, 92, 301
Reform, 37, 38, 142
Reform movement, 37, 38
Reform order, 38
Regerings Reglement, 18-19
Regional, 7, 9, 106, 214, 215
Regional Representative Council, 9
Registered letter, 334
Registration, 22, 92, 95, 97, 98, 121, 123, 142, 184, 187, 188, 195, 252-257, 259, 262, 263, 278, 287, 294, 298, 301
Reglement op de Strafvordering, 22
Regulation(s), 22, 24, 26, 28, 30, 36, 39, 40, 42, 66, 71, 87, 94, 95, 98, 99, 106, 108, 112, 119, 122, 124, 137, 141, 142, 159, 160, 163, 174, 184, 188, 199, 212, 216, 221, 240, 264, 269, 276, 288, 293, 300, 307, 340
Religion law, 73
Relinquishment, 212, 213, 288, 304
Removal, 288, 317, 339
Rent, 105-106
Repayment, 230, 234, 239, 246, 250, 261-264, 278, 290, 300, 315, 329, 330, 339
Represent, 226, 249
Representative office, 64, 65
Revindicatoir, 324
Revocation, 49, 206-209, 211-213, 304
Right, 167, 341-345
Right and obligation, 40
- right of lease, 60, 65, 164, 168, 170–172

Right of management, 109, 111, 117, 126
- right of ownership, 60, 61, 98, 109, 111, 117, 125, 126, 187, 212, 258, 325
- right of use, 60, 64
- right to build, 60, 63, 108–111, 117, 126, 212
- right to collect forest' production, 59
- right to cultivate, 58–60, 62, 103, 108, 117, 212
- right to open land, 60, 66

Roman, 230, 232, 238
Round Table Conference, 27
Roya parsial, 277

Security, 50, 114-123, 181-184, 214, 215, 222, 230-348
Separatist creditor, 309
Shareholder, 154, 184, 202, 203, 276, 295, 302
Shares, 119, 154, 164, 184, 202, 295
Ship, 22, 121, 240
Soil, 57, 90, 198
Source, 41-43, 136, 176
Staatsblad, 71-73, 115, 275
State budget, 205
State of the Republic of Indonesia, 7
State-owned enterprises, 204, 205, 215
Statute, 43, 165, 166, 346-348
Stock exchange, 264
Student, 37
Subjective law, 40
Subrogation, 301
Supersemar, 34
Supreme Court, 10, 100, 197, 285, 328
Surveying, 92

Tangible, 55, 118, 143, 144, 154, 180, 183, 239, 241, 312, 321-323
Temporary Constitution of 1950
- temporary right, 29

Tenants, 90, 173, 211, 288
Term, 5, 8, 35, 43, 75, 141, 162, 166, 169, 216, 244, 280, 288, 313, 329, 331
Testament, 78, 80, 89
Testator, 76, 79, 81
Third party
- tithing, 49, 58, 59

Title, 22, 39, 74, 76, 83-89, 126, 145, 151, 153, 161, 186, 194, 219, 233, 238, 263,

264, 266, 267, 274, 276, 286, 288, 289, 291, 297, 301, 304, 309, 313, 324, 332
Trade, 11–13, 86, 154, 164, 175, 264, 331
Tradeable, 265
Transfer, 89, 92, 96, 98, 106, 117, 149, 161, 174, 185–188, 219, 221, 230, 234–236, 239, 241, 259, 260, 268, 284, 295, 301–303, 314–315, 317, 318, 321, 328, 330, 334
Treasure hall, 188
Trust, 44–50, 78–82, 99, 222–230, 232, 234, 235, 239
Trustee, 197, 249

Unitary, 7, 27, 29, 138, 338
Unitary State of the Republic of Indonesia unity, 29
Unity in diversity, 4
Unregistered land, 187, 286, 297
Urban, 131–142
Usufruct, 101

Valid, 24, 26, 28, 31, 32, 80, 223, 318, 345
Vereenigde Oost Indische Compagnie Era (VOC), 11–15
Virtue of law, 131, 187, 259, 260, 301, 309, 332
VOC. *See* Vereenigde Oost Indische Compagnie Era (VOC)
Void, 76, 140, 174, 261, 265, 288, 289, 297, 299, 304, 309, 321, 328
Voluntary, 212, 226, 227, 288, 304, 305, 308, 339
Voting rights, 295
Vruchtgebruik, 49

Water, 48, 49, 56, 108, 133, 214
Wetboek van Koophandel, 22
Wetboek van Strafrecht, 22
Will, 280
Written off, 305

Zaakgevolg, 284
Zaakwaarneming, 224

Made in the USA
Monee, IL
13 September 2026

62974278R00070